CW01262345

Dedication

For Janet, Elisabeth and Meriel

SOMEONE ELSE'S STORY

Two members of the salvage team on Rona 1941

SOMEONE ELSE'S STORY

STORIES FROM THE HEBRIDES AS RE-TOLD
BY **MICHAEL ROBSON**

acair

Registered Charity SC047866

First published in 2018 by Acair, An Tosgan, Seaforth Road,
Stornoway, Isle of Lewis, Scotland HS1 2SD

www.acairbooks.com
info@acairbooks.com

Text © the Estate of Michael Robson, 2018

The right of Michael Robson to be identified as the author of the work has been asserted by them in accordance with the Copyright, Designs and Patent Act 1998.

All rights reserved.
No part of this publication may be reproduced, stored in a retrieval system nor reproduced or transmitted by any means, electronic, mechanical, photocopying or otherwise, without the prior permission of the publisher.

Cover and interior design by Joan MacRae-Smith for Acair

A CIP catalogue record for this title is available from the British Library

Printed by Hobbs, Hampshire, England

ISBN 978-1-78907-015-6

Published in collaboration with Comunn Eachdraidh Nis, 2018

Contents

Acknowledgements		8
Illustrations		9
Abbreviations		11
Foreword		13
Preface		14
Michael Robson 1933-2017		15
Chapter I	On the rapid stream of time	17
Chapter II	Clach an Truiseil	43
Chapter III	A Walk from Tolsta to Ness in the 1850s	66
Chapter IV	Dòmhnull Cam	107
Chapter V	Plane lands on Rona	150
Chapter VI	Airidh na h-Aon Oidhche	164
Chapter VII	Alexander Carmichael writes to John A Harvie-Brown	197
Chapter VIII	Letters from John Finlayson	255
Michael Robson	*Island Visits 1948-1992*	339
Publications	*Books and Booklets*	342
Articles		344
Bibliography		348
Index		353

Acknowledgements

In preparing this small book I have relied greatly on the help generously given by Roger Atkinson, Chris Barrowman, Anne Campbell, Armand and Ginette de Mestral, Douglas McLellan, Finlay Macleod, Mary Macleod, Murdo Macleod, David Roberts, Colin Ross, Angus Smith and Norman Smith; and by the staff of the Library (Special Collections) of the University of Edinburgh, the National Library of Scotland, the Library of the National Museums of Scotland, Orkney Archives, and of the Western Isles Library Service in Stornoway. I am no less appreciative of the invaluable interest and work of authors, surveyors, map-makers and local inheritors of traditional knowledge, now of earlier times, on which I have so abundantly depended.

Illustrations

Frontispiece: Two members of the salvage team on Rona 1941 (see Chapter V)

The buildings visited by F W L Thomas in north Harris c.1857, as they are today (see p.21)

Clach an Truiseil – a painting of c.1833 (see p.46) [From Seaton opp. p. 34]

Map: OS 6in 185 : Early stage of the walk from Tolsta (see p.77)

Caisteal a' Mhorair, Tràigh Geiraha, a short way north of Tolsta (see p.83) [Phot. James Smith]

Map: OS 6in Late stage of the walk near Cuidhaseadair (see p.94)

Stac Dhòmhnuill Chaim (see p.110) [Phot. James Smith]

The salvage team outside the cookhouse, Rona (see p.162) [from Alexander Carmichael's collection : Carmina Gadelica vol.vi]

Salvage team on watch practice, armed and ready to defend the island (see p.163)

Map of Benbecula 1822, with 'Watching of One Night' to left of 'Ruevaul' (see p.165)

Site of Airidh na h-Aon Oidhche, Benbecula (see p.175) [Phot. Armand de Mestral]

Loch Airidh na h-Aon Oidhche, in South Lochs (see p.176)

Highlander threatened by a black dog. (see p.177)

Loch Airidh na h-Aon Oidhche, in the Bragar moor (see p.189) [Phot. Anne Campbell]

Black Rats (see p.248) [From Harvie-Brown & Buckley opp. p.36a]

Alexander Finlayson (centre), doctor at Munlochy, Black Isle (see p.256)

Cliffs of Lianamull, Mingulay (etched from a photograph by W Norrie) (see p.273) [From Harvie-Brown & Buckley opp. p.162]

Ruins of Torwood Castle, supposed to resemble in design the ancient house of Dunipace. Drawn by Miss Sherriff (see p.284) [From John C Gibson opp. p.130]

The house of Dunipace, renovated after the fire of 1897 and drawn later by Miss Sherriff, Carronvale (see p.300) [From John C Gibson opp. p.84]

Abbreviations

The abbreviations listed below relate to the sources and references given at the end of each chapter:

CWC	Carmichael Watson Collection
NLS	National Library of Scotland
NRS	National Records of Scotland
OS	Ordnance Survey
OSA	The First or Old Statistical Account of Scotland
OSNB	Ordnance Survey Name Book
P.S.A.S.	Proceedings of the Society of Antiquaries of Scotland
RCAHMCS	The Royal Commission on Ancient and Historical Monuments & Constructions of Scotland
SG	*Stornoway Gazette* [NLS annotated copy]
TGSI	Transactions of the Gaelic Society of Inverness

Foreword

This new book by Michael Robson is a miscellany of gems of island history. The topics are wide-ranging, including tales about the terror inflicted upon Lewis in the seventeenth century by Dòmhnall Cam MacDhùghail, traditions about Clach an Truiseil and Àirigh na h-Aon Oidhche and an account of a plane landing on North Rona in 1941. The chapters containing letters from Alexander Carmichael and John Finlayson to the leading ornithologist of his time, John A Harvie-Brown, are particularly fascinating. The great store of knowledge of the natural world demonstrated by Carmichael and Finlayson is highly impressive.

Carmichael's use of the phrase 'floating on the rapid stream of time' reflects the urgency with which he went about his work of collecting folklore and Gaelic words and phrases. There was so much to gather, and time was limited. His account of obtaining 400-500 lines of poetry and the 'Hymn of Christ' in 1869 from Donald Macdonald, a six year old boy in South Uist, shows the rich and wonderful vein of tradition available to Carmichael and other collectors at that time.

As usual, Michael is meticulous with oral and written sources and cross-references. He is highly skilled in comparing and contrasting different versions of events and tales, leaving his readers to come to their own conclusions.

The book is very informative and well written and I know that it will appeal to a wide readership.

Iain G Macdonald, Habost, Ness

Preface

The contents of the following eight chapters of this book have happened to catch the attention of the author at one time or another, much as the attention of Arthur Mitchell was caught by the *craggan* he saw beside the stone-breaker sitting at the edge of the road to Barvas. They are only a tiny fraction of the mass of incidental intriguing interest offered by the people, the landscape and the seas of the Outer Hebrides, the discovery and adventure of which are so well expressed in the following salutary words from Alexander Carmichael's introduction to *Carmina Gadelica*:

> *This work consists of old lore collected during the last forty-four years. It forms a small part of a large mass of oral literature written down from the recital of men and women throughout the Highlands and Islands … Some of the tales however, are long, occupying a night or even several nights in recital. '***Sgeul Coise Cèin***', the story of the foot of Cian, for example, was in twenty-four parts, each part occupying a night in telling …*
>
> *Three sacrifices have been made – the sacrifice of time, the sacrifice of toil, and the sacrifice of means. These I do not regret. I have three regrets – that I have not been earlier collecting, that I have not been more diligent in collecting, and that I am not better qualified to treat what I have collected …*
>
> *These notes and poems have been an education to me. And so have been the men and women reciters from whose dictation I wrote them down. They are almost all dead now, leaving no successors.*

Michael Robson 1933-2017

Michael John Harvey Robson was born in Cullercoats, near Whitley Bay, Northumberland, on 29 August 1933. He attended Hexham Primary School, Northumberland, from 1939 to 1946, and Canford School, Wimborne, Dorset from 1946 to 1951.
Michael undertook his National Service in the Royal Artillery (Gunners) from 1952 to 1954, where he saved enough money to pay his way through university. In 1958 he graduated MA (Hons) in English from the University of Edinburgh.

He began his teaching career in 1959 at Galashiels Academy where he remained for a year. In 1960 he moved to George Watson's College, Edinburgh, where he taught English. From all accounts, he was an inspirational and charismatic teacher who was much loved and respected by his pupils. During his time at Watson's, Michael was involved in three school trips to St Kilda. On the first trip in 1966 the school party's departure from the island was delayed by four days due to bad weather.

From 1976 to 1982 Michael was Curator at Wilton Lodge Museum in Hawick. This provided better access to his on-going studies of Borders farming and local history. While in this post he was responsible for several initiatives, such as the project to research the prehistoric aurochs, an extinct species of large wild cattle that inhabited Europe, Asia, and North Africa, found on Synton Moss, and the important and pioneering archaeological dig at Priesthaugh in Teviothead. His work there also paved the way towards the development of the Liddesdale Heritage Association in Newcastleton which was born out of a small Local History Group.

which was done, with illustrations, by Mitchell himself in a book published seventeen years after his first sight of them. What seems now more important by far is the mixed sense of shock and privilege which must have been felt by Mitchell and Thomas as they happened to look at the man sitting on the ground at the roadside, not only because he was having a rest from breaking stones to one of the regulation sizes required for road construction but especially because he was eating from an apparently ancient vessel. On such moments, hastily noted down afterwards, the track of life can feel as if it has been altered for ever.

❖

Before leaving the two travellers to continue their journey it is worth considering why Mitchell found it an advantage to have the company of Captain Thomas. Was there anything, in 1863, special about Thomas?

 By whatever naval rank he was known, and as time had gone by it had quite naturally changed in accordance with gradual promotion, Thomas had spent several years in the service of the Hydrographic Survey along the west coast of the Outer Hebrides, more particularly in the area adjacent to Harris and south-west Lewis. As 'Commander Thomas' on a survey vessel he had been busy charting the ocean depths around Taransay, West Loch Tarbert and the narrow Loch Resort in or about 1857, not long before he managed a voyage to St Kilda. When at sea somewhere near Gàisgeir he must have frequently gazed at the bare, rough and rocky shores of the islands, and the wild hills that rose behind them. Perhaps he had imagined at first that he was looking at an uninhabited country which had the appearance of being so inhospitable that no family would have been able to find a foothold for a dwelling and no cow or sheep a suitable patch of grass worth grazing.

Mentioning later, without stating the year, that 'I was stationed last summer on the borders of the Forest of Harris, – a mountainous region bare of trees', Thomas told how he had discovered here and there, surely to his surprise, 'abundance of excellent pasture', much of which probably lay at the back of white beaches of fine sand and in hollows or on low slopes not obvious from his ship. In due course he made a visit to Tarbert and took photographs of thatched buildings there and ragged looking children, and this could have been on the occasion when he seems to have sailed in to West Loch Tarbert as far as the entrance to 'Loch Meabhag', which he called 'a narrow creek running five-sixths of a mile into the land'. From a distance at least 'a solitary gamekeeper's lodge' was 'the only sign of human life' around the 'creek'.[2]

Apart from his exploring of Tarbert, which may have been on a different day, Thomas also went ashore – probably at Tolmachan on the opposite side of the loch from Miabhaig itself – and it was perhaps the gamekeeper there who informed him 'that on the moor, about half a mile from the head of this loch, there was a circular house, roofed entirely with stone and without a bit of wood in its construction'. Now Thomas, whose earlier connections were primarily with Orkney, was clearly interested already in ancient stone structures and may have read about those to be seen in the south-west of Ireland. Certainly, on being told there was one near Miabhaig, though in fact rather more than a mile up into 'the moor' and of a kind that he knew almost nothing about, his curiosity was greatly aroused and he set off eagerly to find it. This he failed to do, and it was on a second search that he discovered not one but 'two beehive-houses', one complete, the other partly ruinous. He realised that it was not surprising that he had missed them on the first occasion as they were 'hardly to be distinguished from the granite blocks around'.

It was only two or three years later that Dr Mitchell had Thomas for company as they drove, or walked, from Uig to Barvas. Perhaps indeed the track of the latter's life had only recently been altered by that day, or two or three days, at Miabhaig and on the edge of the mountains of north Harris. With a naval career that had 'stationed' him in the area and with opportunity for a break from navigation and soundings at sea, Thomas could well have felt that it was a suitable time to follow up his interest in antiquities. But if speculation is appropriate at this point, there are several possible reasons for guessing that the dominating enthusiasm of his subsequent years began in the summer of 1856 or 1857 in the Forest of Harris.

His Royal Navy or Hydrographic duties did not give way entirely to his archaeological and historical pursuits at this stage, but that these pursuits somehow caught fire about thirty years before his death in 1886 seems evident. To what cause can this be attributed, or rather, to stretch the speculation a degree further, at what point in his visit to north Harris did Thomas feel that an absorbing interest could have taken control of his spare time? If it happened during those few summer days, was it due to the rugged, mysterious hills and glens of Harris, to a meeting with a local gamekeeper, to a walk up to a secretive, bouldery shelf of green pasture below a looming cliff, to a small, circular building amazingly entire and utterly ancient in appearance, or to information supplied that same evening by 'my assistant, Mr Morrison, a native of Lewis'? Any one, or a combination of any number, of these encounters might have been the key, the unexpected fleeting moment that opened up a new and exciting world.

❖

Within a year or so, Thomas landed again, with a remarkable Lewis expedition in mind. He might have come ashore from his ship on the north side of Loch Resort, or with equal convenience on the south-east shore of Loch Tamanabhaigh or near the head of Loch Tealasbhaigh. But he decided to approach from the Uig road, wild as it was at that time, and to walk south and west into the moor, leaving all roads far behind as he would have done if approaching from the Tamanabhaigh direction. This time he brought with him 'my assistant Mr Sharbau', a draughtsman on the survey vessel, whose surname, because it was written in a hand which, like many at the time and earlier, tended to make 'u' and 'n' look much the same, could have been 'Sharban'. Recollecting all his Harris experience from two years previously, and his anticipation filling his imagination with what his 'assistant', Mr Morrison, had told him about the 'beehive-houses' in Uig, Thomas and Sharbau made their way 'on a dark and cheerless day in August' to where, with the aid of

Buildings visited by F W L Thomas in North Harris c1857, as they are today

a copy of the Ordnance Survey map published just about five years previously, they felt was the appropriate starting point for setting off to find more of the sort of ancient dwellings already discovered above Miabhaig.

Rather vaguely, without supplying either place-name or exact location, Thomas began his record of the day in a thatched structure evidently inhabited: 'On the road we had been resting in one of these archaic homes; seated upon the bench before the little fire, and out of the cold wind, I can answer that I found it very comfortable.' Not so comfortable at all were the next miles into the wilds, 'when the wet was splashing from the moor at every step', until at length after crossing the great spaces of Maghannan the two men reached what they called 'the Bushy Lake', probably Loch na Craobhaig, from which they 'strolled up the burn of Fidigidh' until they came 'to the object of our search'. Here, in a striking scene, were about twenty ancient dwellings of varied shape, some of them 'beehive' and many of them occupied as shielings, with cattle grazing round about. Thomas and his assistant sat down, Sharbau made the first of his sketches, and eventually, when he had finished drawing, they moved on to the extremity of their walk and without doubt the climax of their expedition.[3]

To someone like Thomas, already absorbed in reflections on how such remarkable, unexpected and simple buildings had come to exist in a wild and beautiful country, that August day should have been unforgettable and have haunted the memory of the two 'Hydrographic' surveyors. If he had wanted to impress a fellow antiquarian who had never imagined that witnessing such scenes was possible in Britain, Thomas would have tried to arrange another visit as soon as possible, to reassure himself that what he had experienced was not a dream and to introduce a different companion who, once he had overcome his initial astonishment, might have some fascinating theories of his own. But it was some time before he was able to do this.

Such had been his antiquarian interest that Thomas became a communicating member of the Society of Antiquaries in Scotland and adopted a more confident and authoritative attitude in this aspect of his life. He therefore seemed to keep himself apart from those inhabitants of the Lewis parishes who could have told him so much, referring to them collectively as 'the natives', and as a naval officer he remained in a superior position relative to the ordinary members of the crew on board the survey vessels. Some at least of his 'assistants' helped in a search of south-west Harris for early stone houses, and when one was found half-buried under sand a team of 'my people' became a labour force and 'turned to with a will to excavate it, a work of great labour to any but a professional navigator'. Nearby was 'a simple massive pillar, 11 feet high, sacred to the memory of some unknown saint or warrior', but, according to Thomas, 'It never enters the minds of the degenerate islanders that ordinary heads and hands could carry and upraise such stupendous blocks'. It was a characteristic of people like Thomas, Mitchell and other authorities in some field, as of many schoolteachers, that they should be definite in their pronouncements and certain in their identifications, and this was what was expected of them as those who were supposed to 'know the answers'.

Thomas thus made the acquaintance of others of his kind and of the few such 'authoritative' figures to be met in the Outer Hebrides when he was there. In the late 1850s he probably made contact with T S Muir, who was then keenly investigating the remains of early ecclesiastical structures, old chapels and churches to be found all around the islands, even on the remotest, and who took more than a passing interest in those ruins that could be declared to be 'archaic'. An appropriate meeting place was the Society of Antiquaries, a close-knit network chiefly of professional gentlemen who were, or liked to believe themselves to be, scholarly researchers entitled to consider themselves leaders in archaeology and so on, and to mix with each other through publishing learned articles. In these circumstances, there would be every probability that Commander, later Captain, Thomas and Dr Mitchell should communicate with each other and, late in 1862 or a few months after, arrange to make an expedition together to Lewis so that Thomas could at last show off his discoveries in some of the remotest corners of the island.

❖

Before March 1867, and probably in 1863, Thomas did meet up with Mitchell in Lewis and walked to the head of Loch Resort. According to Thomas's account they spent a while in the surrounding area:

'Being Sunday-stayed, along with Dr A Mitchell, at Ken Resort, we thought to improve the occasion by visiting the garrys in the neighbourhood. Along with the gamekeeper and a gentleman known through all these bounds, we were soon at Larach Tigh Dhubhastail … Here was a bo'h, in which the family was at home. This was the garry or summer pasturage of the tenants of Crolista, twelve miles away on the borders of Loch Roag.'[4]

From Làrach Taigh Dhubhastail Thomas and Mitchell may well have visited more 'garrys' and then set out westwards across the moor on more or less the same path as Thomas had followed with Sharbau a few years earlier. It seems quite likely that this latest joint venture into the moors and mountains of Uig was the reason for the two men being on the road out of Uig when they saw the stone-breaker and went off with his craggan. As collectors they had actually paid for their trophy, which was not always what happened in such situations. One reason for their intended visit to Barvas, which was not on the most direct route to Stornoway, their eventual destination, could have been to see for themselves if what Thomas had been told about the people there was true, although a centre of craggan making would be an added incentive to go there.

'The district of Barvas in Lewis is, by the Lewis people themselves, considered to be inhabited by a race distinct from those in the rest of the island – that is, they are dark, short, square, ugly, large-bellied, and with much cunning under a foolish exterior; they are said to be more backward than the rest, so that the "Taobh s'iar" (Taobh n'iar), "west side," which does not include Uig, is proverbially connected with dirt and slovenliness. In this part of Lewis alone remains the custom of leaving a hole in the thickness of the wall for a dormitory ..'[5]

Perhaps Thomas wanted to see the hole in the wall where they slept, rather than the people who lived in such conditions.

❖

It happened, however, that soon after his earlier expeditions and his journey with Dr Mitchell, Thomas heard about a new and different kind of authority on the Hebrides, one who was not a member of the Society of Antiquaries and whose experience of those who were had not been so far very pleasing. This was Alexander Carmichael, who stemmed from the island of Lismore and in 1867 had been living for some time in Lochmaddy. He was already deeply interested in the traditions and antiquities of the Outer Hebrides, partly perhaps because he may have read various antiquarian articles, including those of Thomas on the 'beehive houses', and had tried to produce one or two such accounts himself.

Chapter I

More important than articles, however, Carmichael was busy noting down intriguing pieces of information picked up from people he chanced to meet in Uist and Benbecula; and he was in touch with Thomas who, he thought, must share his interest in his discoveries. In January 1867 he wrote to Thomas that 'I have filled several sheets of foolscap on antiquarian matters' and 'I am waiting time to add more'. But he was wary of learned contributors to the Society of Antiquaries, so he added cautiously: 'The antiquities of these islands are really interesting and the more they are investigated the more interesting they become. As I told you before I know but little of antiquities.'[6] And in a lengthy letter to Thomas of 28 March in the same year he made his position clearer, and strikingly so:

'I am looking forward with very great Interest indeed to your forthcoming memoir on the ancient duns of the Outer Hebrides. I will be delighted if anything I can send will be of service to you. I hope I need hardly assure you of this. I am deeply interested in everything which concerns the Highlands and Islands and he who honestly endeavours to throw light upon the ancient habits and customs of these can at all times command my willing services to the extent of my humble abilities.

'I am so much in the habit of being discouraged in prosecuting my antiquarian predilections that your kind words of encouragement are to me what the shower is to the parched plant of summer. Those old people with the marvellous memories are the only parties from whom I have been in the habit of receiving any sympathy or cooperation. And this sympathy is perhaps all the more genuine because we are both proscribed – they openly and I silently.

'For the last seven years I have been doing all in my power to rescue from oblivion things which I found floating on the rapid stream of time.'[7]

It was such floating things that were to determine the main course of Carmichael's active life over the next thirty or more years; and antiquities, a subject belonging, it seemed to him, more appropriately to an academic and somewhat exclusive social sphere, were to become for him a rather peripheral pursuit even though that sphere offered a means of acquiring for the knowledge of the 'old people with the marvellous memories', and for himself, greater scholarly and social credibility. But those chance pieces of knowledge – place names, songs, stories, charms, sayings, historical and genealogical fragments, knowledge of settlements, objects and surroundings – all remembered, told and heard in the course of days and nights, were part of 'an immense mass of traditional lore floating among the old people of these Islands'. To find that 'mass' ignored and, as the years went by, disappearing rapidly with the passing of old people around him, shocked and saddened Carmichael as he came to realise the amazing wealth of knowledge preserved in the memories of those who were too often dismissed as ignorant peasants. He hoped that Thomas might help in the rescue task, even if by recording only a tiny portion of the wealth which survived in a quantity which Carmichael described as still immense. 'I am of opinion,' he told Thomas, 'that by diligent and persevering search two hundred volumes as large as the Waverley Novels could be collected in South Uist and Barra alone.' After all, 'I know several old men there from whom I have taken down old tales, who have often assured me that they would keep me writing constantly for two months.'[8]

What sort of things could be caught before they disappeared for ever with the death of someone on a neighbouring island or just a short way down the road? Another letter from Carmichael, written on 19 November 1866, mentioned a few of them which Thomas might have come across but had probably not realised were at hand:

of modern thought and enlightenment. The young are taught to despise "folk-lore" and to condemn the old who recite it. Consequently "folk-lore" will in a few years be "stamped out" and be a thing of the past. But if those who condemn the old people were to go more among them and know them better I feel sure they would be more tolerant towards them. Nay more, I am satisfied that as they became more impressed as they would inevitably become, with the great natural intelligence wondrously retentive memories and thoroughly gentlemanly demeanour of these old people they would become their friends instead of being their foes.

'For myself I love these old people more than I care to say. It may be questionable weakness on my part, but I always feel when one of them dies as if I had lost a dear and sympathetic friend.'[11]

However, all was not lost. Carmichael came across some of the younger generation who had indeed learned things from their elders, children who had sat quietly in the background and pleased fathers and grandfathers, mothers and grandmothers, with what they remembered, or had been taught:

'I took down several versions of the beautiful poem of *Fraoch* in Argyle and the Outer Isles. They all agree in the main but differ in detail. That, however, which I like best is a version written on the 7th April 1869 from the recitation of a remarkable boy six years of age, Donald Macdonald, son of Alexander Macdonald, crofter Snaoisval, South Uist. Probably I took down in all from 400 to 500 lines of excellent old poetry from this wonderful child of song modesty and memory.

'Among other things was a hymn which the boy called the "Hymn of Christ". This resembles and may actually be a free rendering of the hymn of Saint Bernard entitled - . If it be a free rendering of the Latin of Saint Bernard the Gaelic to my thinking is infinitely finer than the English translation beautiful as that is.

There is a dignity and grandeur about the Gaelic unapproached by the English version.

'The only difficulty experienced with this boy was childlike, his disposition to gambol about with his companions. There were a kitten, a pup and a lamb in the house and every now and then these three and the boy rose and had a frolic on the floor together.

'The boy's grandfather Donl mac an taillear – Donald son of the tailor – a nice old man – sat in a corner enveloped in friendly peat smoke and now and again scolded the boy in a friendly way for not attending to the gentleman.

'At last, fairly tired and done up these four young playful delightful and frolicsome creatures lay down on the floor beside the friendly fire of peats and nestled in one round group as if they were one family and fell fast asleep. A shaggy little six-horned sheep an equally shaggy symmetrical black calf and a sturdy ragged little foal all [at?] times and sometimes together looked in and sniffed the nestling group beside the fire. The writer too, tired and fatigued, drew his cloak over him and stretching himself on the wooden bench Gaelic *seist*, on which he sat, fell fast asleep and slept soundly till the cold awoke him in the grey dawn of the morning. Leaving the house as quietly as he could, he washing himself in the fresh friendly stream, he walked on several miles to the house of one of his innumerable kind and most hospitable friends where he had breakfast.'

And as an important afterthought, Carmichael repeated a most significant sentence: 'One of the things obtained from this child was *Laoidh Chriosd* the Lay or Hymn of Christ, probably one of the finest sacred poems in the Gaelic language.'[12]

What a day was that, the 7th April 1869!

❖

Chapter I

The correspondence between Carmichael and Thomas continued from the mid 1860s for another ten or so years, no doubt to the mutual benefit of both. Each produced the text of proposed articles or essays and sent it for comment and correction by the other, Thomas showing a stricter attitude towards his task. For example, when checking a manuscript from Carmichael on the Outer Hebrides, he observed in his critical, authoritative tone:

> 'Lews. Lews is an abomination; there is no authority for it. The real name is Leoghas = the Marshy-Land. And Lewis is the name of the whole island, of which Harris, in Gaelic Na h' Arduibh = The Heights (of Lewis), is a natural district.
>
> "Caolas Iorst". There is no rst in Gaelic. If you wish to convey the sound, write Caolas h – Iart (pro. Kuaolas Hirst). The oldest written form is Hirta (pro. Hirsta), probably for Iar-tir, meaning the West-Land or country. How can Caolas, which means a narrow sound, be applied to North Uist?'[13]

Neither Carmichael nor Thomas were always right!

In the same way, Carmichael always seems to have talked with and learned from the ordinary 'peasant' folk; Thomas seldom did, preferring to acquire information from schoolteachers, ministers, and 'Society' men like Dr Mitchell, though occasionally from Alexander Carmichael. However, Thomas did make notes of certain things which probably struck him as of special interest and worth recording, though it appears that he had not necessarily received them from original sources. A brief 'list' in his handwriting of such fleeting pieces of traditional knowledge, part of which is given below, falls far short of the great mass of information kept on random paper sheets and scraps by Carmichael, though this is not to deny that there is considerable value in the results of Thomas's enquiries and in the articles he published on Hebridean subjects. His list included, first of all, the following sixteen or seventeen items, which related to the traditional and historical owners or lairds of Lewis, and probably derived from Angus Gunn, the cottar in North Dell, Ness. It began with the very word of which, elsewhere, Thomas had greatly disapproved:

Lews (d)

1. *The first inhabitants were sent from Lochlin by King Donmarag (? Denmark); they found only an old woman with two sheep at North Galson*
2. *King Magnus of Lochlin – who was not the son of King Donmarag – lived and died at Castle Magnus, near the well, between Eorobe and Habost*
3. *Sileas, a relative of Magnus, came from Lochlin, but claiming Harris, he was killed – and buried at the March (boundary) of Harris; he left a natural son, who did not succeed*
4. *After the death of Sileas, (the Uachdaran or Govenor) the first McLeod came from Lochlin. He was no relative; he lived at "Mac Leods Castle" at Eorobe, of which there are some remains*
5. *Then came Torquil Heir Mac Leod's eldest natural son; he reigned for about 60 years. The inhabitants of Lewis were then few. The first Macaulays came from Lochlin and settled in Uig when the first Mac Leod came. Torquil Heir had three brothers; two were lairds at Ullapool and the third Murdo was drowned at Strath Leod, at Skye. The two brothers got Donald Cam*

Chapter I

Macaulay and Dearg, a ship-captain, to forcefully take Torquil Heir from Loch Carloway to Ullapool., where he was killed in the night-time by the wife of one of the brothers. The people who suspected the two brothers, would not

6. *submit to them; they made Murdo Morrison, who was descended from the first inhabitants who came from Lochlin, Proprietor and Judge. He was the first Judge in Ness and was always called <u>The</u> Judge; he was married to an Irish lady, lived at Habost and was killed at Ullapool by a former admirer of his wife*

7. *He had four sons Allan, Donald, Kenneth and Angus, who were joint Proprietors and Judges: the remains of their four houses are pointed out by the old people, but there is no account of their having descendants. The Castle of Stornoway is supposed to have been built about this time*

8. *Their only sister married the son (Caen) of the Laird of Ardnamurchan. Caen lived at Habost and became Proprietor and Judge – he was blind some years before his death. He had two sons*

9. *Donald and Macgillemhor (Morrison) who were joint Proprietors and Judges. Donald having no family, the brothers were succeeded by*

10. *Donald, the son of Macgillemhor; there is no account of his having a family*

11. *It was in his time that the Mackenzie came to the island; the Macdonald was making war on the Lews, when Donald Macgillemhor craved the assistance of Mackenzie (the "soldier" or "victorious") of Kintail, promising one half of the Lews for his help. [Marginal note by Thomas: <u>Soldier</u> – a mistake for <u>Tutor</u>] Mackenzie promised part of Kintail to Donald, but never gave it. It is not known if Donald had any family, but on the death of Donald the "Soldier of Kintail" took the whole island, paying*

nothing for it. He was the first that put on any rent; 6d for a cow, 6d for a horse, 2d for a sheep and lamb, 1d for a single sheep

12. *William Mor, his son, succeeded him (Kenneth): he it was who increased the rent to 15 shillings for a half-penny land; North Galson was a five-penny land, and the rent of South Galson was £3 a year. William was found dead at Stornoway.*
    (There must be a gap here of one or two proprietors but their names are unknown)
13. *Mackenzie "the Little" succeeded, supposed to have been a grandson of William Mor*
14. *His cousin Francis succeeded; – Francis the Deaf, (Bodhar)*
15. *His daughter, Mrs Stewart Mackenzie, succeeded*
16. *Sir James Matheson, Bart., who alone paid any money for the Lews*

Stornoway Castle was built soon after the emigration from Lochlin. The sons of the Judge had a house near the Old Castle of Stornoway which seemingly ? was built before the Castle.

It is to be regretted that after hearing many stories, mixed with a great deal of superstition (sufficient if written to make a volume), from Angus Gunn, North Dale, the above alone could be picked out as bearing on the point. No dates – unable to write. – Norman Macleod, the Bard, would no doubt be able to give much information, but as he is said to draw on his imagination in prose as well as in poetry, his truthfulness is sometimes suspected. I asked Donald Morrison to write something, and his writings are enclosed.

[Corrected note: The above probably from Rev. John Macrae, Stornoway (Mr Strachan, Barvas – deleted)]

Chapter I

Next was a short list of Mackenzie owners of Lewis, and this was succeeded by the names of ministers for the four Lewis parishes. There was then a series of short remarks on aspects of sea fisheries:

The curing of cod and ling in Ness 60 years ago (1857)

Curer was Mc Ivor Bs father

Nothing but hand-lines and the Parish smith made the hooks. Dogfish bounty – and paid rent

Loch Roag – herrings first

Curing of herrings began about [blank] : great work

Curing at Ness 36 years; long lines

Mr R Morrison, the bankers grandfather, first curer of herrings died 1790; cured say 30 years before; lived in Tanga in Stornoway, but his widow died; traded extensively ? in Stornoway

Pier at Ness built about 20 years ago [House?] built in 1791

The preceeding notes are copied from papers written by the Revd. Mr Gunn, Minister of Uig, and were sent to me by his widow, March, 1861.

The 'preceeding notes' were those about the Mackenzie owners and the parish ministers. Finally the paper came to an end with a variety of items possibly noted by Thomas but sketchy sources for these were given in only five instances:

Gaelic Proverb – "It is his own child the Priest christens first"

Loch Resort – is named in a novel, called St Clair of the Isles, by Eliz. Helme.

St Kilda – "His like cannot be found from Hirt to Pirt (Hirst to Pirst) i.e. between St. Kilda and Perth.

White-Livered. A superstition common to Lewis and Germany is that when a man or woman becomes a widower or widow twice or thrice it is because he or she is "white-livered". A learned Lewis doctor, at Scarp, was able to recognise the wife of a man who was causing her husbands illness; but a knowing hand in another case avoided any evil consequences by eschewing all conjugal duty "in bed".

Mac Naughtens sometimes called Mac Nicols in Lewis.

Fosterage. It was an honour to be a fosterer and prized. Macdonald of Berneray (Lewis) was fostered in a family till he grew to be a lad [was old enough to go to school – deleted], when he was removed to another family from which he could attend school. Macdonald had a "black" still in Berneray. It happened that both his foster-fathers visited him at the same time; he set a cog of whiskey before them, and knowing they would fall out, he left them to drink and quarrel in comfort. Their conversation was of course in praise of their ward, but each claimed to be superiour in the "making" of him. "It is I who made him what he is; it was with me he got his education." "What of that" replied the other, who had had charge of him when an infant; "it is I who made a man of him." Now Macdonald had grown only to a fat and stuffy figure, so the school-fosterer retorted; "And you have not finished your work yet." This was not to be borne, and to blows they went. J. M.

Chapter I

Macleod Gentry – Thirty years ago there were 15 gentlemen of the name of Macleod, on Macleod's property in Skye; now there is but one – Orbost. From a lady at Grammarsdale.

Taransay Macdonald's father died worth £1800 – carried his goods from Aberdeen on horseback – dined with Caterans (cattle-stealers) at Carn a Caoran – married a daughter of Campbell of Scalpay – he lost £700 by Macleod of Harris. From Taransay. This family namd by Martin in "Second Sight"; Morrisons Trad. Lewis – and said [to?] be descendants of "Macdonald of the Second Blow". Rev. J. McD. [Harris?]

Kidnapping. Norman Macleod of Berneray, Harris, kidnapped a lot of Harris people, but the ship was obliged to put into Belfast, when they escaped by means of Evander Macleod, by means of an iron bar. Tar.

Burial. People were buried at Uidh, Taransay, until lately, when a coffin was found above ground, <u>which</u> was considered a hint to leave off. J.

Seals. Gaasgeir. Fifteen years since the average crop of seals from Gaasgier was about 30; in Stewarts time, 80 or 90. Loss to Uidh of £12.

Sheep Stealing. 20 sheep were put ashore on Gaasgier in 186[-], but only 5, and 3 lambs were left in autumn.

Potatoe Failure. Taransay yielded 400 barrels of potatoes before the general failure in [blank]; but only 12½ bar. that year. Since then the yield has never been so great as formerly.

Any of the headings in this last section of Thomas's paper, like 'craggan' at the beginning of this chapter, can give rise to recollections, to unusual words heard by chance, to objects seen once and never again. It is well over a century since Thomas wrote the notes about seals on Gàisgeir and about burial at Uidh in Taransay, and it is the same length of years since Carmichael described the 'slabhcan'. It is, he said, 'of a black objectionable appearance, but is immensely relished by all who overcome their first prejudice against it.' And he explained how to prepare it for eating:

'The "slabhcan" is made by boiling the weed in a mixture of common water and the water in which it is itself washed. An addition of a little butter and meal improves it. The best time for gathering the weed is in spring time.'

He added that he had heard that 'an Irish missionary in one of the tenants' houses was given a dish of seaweed called "slabhucan" and barley cakes'.[14]

Has 'slabhcan' become a thing of the past? Perhaps not, and the work that Carmichael set himself may still be possible to continue today. It was less than thirty years ago that a Lewisman described with relish the seaweed and the superficially unappetising dish made from it which he knew as 'slabhcan'. It is the sort of word that could appear in a place-name along the shore, and indeed at the northwest corner of Great Bernera there is a rock slab often under the sea called 'Leac an t Slaucain'.[15] And looking back on Thomas's notes and picking out 'white-livered' was a worthwhile exercise in Scotland no further back in time, and may still be, though perhaps not in Lewis and Germany. But who knows? Who investigates these so-called 'superstitions' now? Many of the chapters in this book, describing walks, places, events, tales and beliefs, illustrate some of the means whereby the unique history and special world of the Outer Hebrides can be explored. But who fills hundreds of sheets of notepaper, as Carmichael did, with the things seen and heard, passing on 'the rapid stream of time'?[16]

References and Notes

1   This episode of the craggan is recorded in the following book – A Mitchell: <u>The Past in the Present: What is Civilisation?</u> Edinburgh 1880 pp.25-32
2   F W L Thomas: 'Notice of beehive houses in Harris and Lewis; with traditions of the "each-uisge," or water-horse, connected therewith' in <u>PSAS</u> Vol.III pp.127-134. Thomas also noted (p.129): 'I did not find any more bothan in the vicinity of Loch Meabhag, but three miles to the westward, near a lake from whence runs Avon Suidh, is the ruin of a both, remarkable for a combination of the circular or beehive house with the oblong square or ordinary form'
3   F W L Thomas: 'Description of beehive houses in Uig, Lewis, and of a Pict's house and cromlech, etc., Harris' in <u>PSAS</u> Vol.III pp.134-144, with illustrative plates
4   F W L Thomas: 'On the primitive dwellings and hypogea of the Outer Hebrides' in <u>PSAS</u> Vol.VII (1870) March 1867 pp.161-162. The well-known gentleman referred to was apparently from Harris; the occupants of the 'bo'h' or shieling 'were under no alarm from us in the company of Mr Macrae of Meabhag'
5   See n.2 p.129
6   <u>CWC</u> LS362 ff.220-221 28 January 1867
7   <u>CWC</u> LS 472 ff.1-12 28 March 1867
8   <u>CWC</u> LS 472 ff.13-15 5 March 1867
9   <u>CWC</u> LS 362 ff.189-190. The loch with the two islands is shown on the modern OS map about half a mile south-west of Flodaigh and named 'Loch na Beire'. There are indeed two islands, one of which is a dun. The island near Nunton called Torcasaidh is in a loch close to the Benbecula west coast. On the island is another dun
10 <u>CWC</u> LS 362 ff.220-221; No.230 The OS map has Màs a'Chnuic north of Ceapabhal, and this may be Carmichael's 'Mas Chaipmheall'
11 <u>CWC</u> LS 472ff.1-12 28 March 1867
12 <u>CWC</u> No.172
13 <u>CWC</u> 472(b) 4 May 1872

14 E Dwelly: <u>The Illustrated Gaelic-English Dictionary</u> Fifth Edition Glasgow 1949 p.848 has slabhagan, being a 'kind of reddish sea weed, an article of food formerly cooked till it dissolved, when it was eaten with bread and butter'. See also slòcan
15 OS 6 ins/1 mile, Sheet 17 (surveyed 1850-53, published 1854)
16 The list by Thomas is among Thomas's papers preserved in the library of the National Museums of Scotland, Chambers Street, Edinburgh

Chapter II
Clach an Truiseil

Between two and three miles north east of Barvas and commanding a wide view out over the shallow valley of the little stream called Feadan Siorravig to the open Atlantic ocean is the solitary standing stone known as Clach an Truiseil. To reach it these days you turn off the main road to Ness in the township of Baile an Truiseil, take a further right-angled turn and walk the last few yards up a slight slope with parallel stone dykes on each side. Lying in the grass is a large, long slab, of the same rock as Clach an Truiseil but nothing like as big. Less than a mile to the south-east is a spot called Steinacleit, while further north is a group of lesser stones on a site also named Steinacleit, where it seems that a circular kerb of boulders encloses the remains of a chambered cairn. Not far away again is another prominent standing stone. Evidently this was an area of conspicuous importance in prehistoric times.

Described in 1914 as a 'magnificent monolith', which it certainly is, Clach an Truiseil can easily be missed today by the vehicle-bound visitor who does not know already of its existence, could only momentarily see it over the higher ground that intervenes between road and stone, and perhaps does not notice the sign and turning. But long ago, in 1695, it attracted the attention of Martin Martin, who either saw it himself or more probably was told about it by a knowledgeable island resident. What Martin had to say about it was that 'The Thrushel Stone in the Parish of Barvas, is above 20 foot high, and almost as much in breadth'. He also remarked of such 'erected Stones' in Lewis

Chapter II

that some of 'the ignorant Vulgar', who when it came to tradition and local information at least were rarely ignorant, told visitors how 'they were Men by Inchantment turn'd into Stones', or, as others asserted, 'they are Monuments of Persons of Note kill'd in Battle'.[1]

❖

These notions about Clach an Truiseil still persisted a century and a half later when they appeared in a description of around 1850, by which time there had long been some doubt about its height:

'A standing stone, nineteen feet above ground, and about three feet square at its base. It is supposed, that there are no less than 12 feet of it Sunk in the ground, which, if true, renders it the longest standing stone in the Lewis. The traditions regarding it are vague and uncertain. Some parties maintain, owing to its resemblance to those at Callanish, that it is a Druidical Erection. Others believe it to have been erected by the Danes, to mark the site of one of their victories.'[2]

Between 1695 and 1850 there were various speculations on the origins and dimensions of this most striking landmark, one of which, dating perhaps to the late 1780s, repeats Martin's record of the belief that it marked the site of some significant incident:

'The custom which prevailed amongst the antient inhabitants of Britain, of erecting stones where a remarkable personage was slain, or in memory of an extraordinary event, has, I presume, been the occasion of the many single stones to be found in the island of Lewis.

'..the most remarkable for size and name, is *Clach an Druidshall*, at Shader, on the west side of Lewis. It stands alone in a muir, and is about sixteen feet high, four broad, and three thick. If we recollect that a third more must be below the surface of the earth, and that it is at least a mile and a half from the shore or any rocky ground, it excites surprise how it could be carried and reared there. That it has been placed there appears from the hollow ground about it, the smaller stones to support it, and the verdure of the earth about its foundation, while the muir surrounding it is covered with heath. No tradition remains of its use.'[3]

The reference here to 'verdure of the earth about its foundation' raises doubts as to whether the writer had ever been to see the stone. In any case moderately early descriptions of mysterious relics surviving from the distant past are frequently reminders of the limitations of the author, and irrespective of whether he had actually visited the subject of his account, his remark that no tradition remained of its use might merely mean that, being in a hurry, he had never heard any tradition. As for the 'verdure' and small supporting stones it seems unlikely that he could have seen either as, judging from slightly later accounts, the lower feet of Clach an Truiseil were concealed by a good depth of peat; and his comment on the absence of any tradition was almost immediately contradicted by the local minister:

'Betwixt Barvas and Strather [Shader], in the middle of a deep moss, where no other stones are to be seen, and at a considerable distance from the sea, there is a very large stone standing upright, called *Clach i Drushel*, famous for nothing but its size, being 18 feet above ground, and 14 feet in circumference, having no figures upon it, as erroneously related. The vulgar tradition concerning it, is too absurd and superstitious to deserve any notice.'[4]

What a pity that the two authors, each intent to hint, through a form of the stone's name, at a connection with druids, should in the first case claim that no tradition existed, and in the second at times taught at a school in Liònal, Ness. From Macphail Murray's contributions reached J F Campbell, who published them in his Leabhar na Feinne: Vol.I Heroic Gaelic Ballads [London 1872 – 'Laoidh an Truisealaich' pp.202-203]. Since the 'Laoidh' is little known the original published version follows in its entirety:

Clach an Truiseil

Laoidh an Truisealaich

'Eisdibh beag ma 's aireamh laoidh,
Chailin O! an stiùir thu mi?

Sgèula leat a Thruiseal mhòir,
Cò na slòigh bh' ann ri d' aois?
Robh thu ann linn nam Fiann?
Am fac thu Fionn, Fial, no Fraoch?

Fraoch mac Chumhail nan cuach òir,
Lèonadh e gun chomhla an airm;
Le biast a ghlinne bho thuath,
Thuit mac Chumhail fo chruaidh cheilg.

Bu mhòr am beud an fhuil bhaor,
Tuiteam le gniomh nam bean baoth;

A cheud là a chaidh Fraoch a shnàmh,
Lu guth mhneimh thàrladh olc;
Thug e làn a bhruit gu tìr,
A chaorrainn abuich mìn gun lochd.

Sud an lus am bheil mo mhian,
A laimh Mhic Chumhail nan ciamh càm
Ubhallan na craoibhe a 's arda dos,
Chi mi air an loch ud thall.

Chapter II

Labhair Mac Chumhail nan cuach,
'S lasair a dhà ghruaidh mar fhuil
Chaidh e shnàmh an loch air uair,
'S an eadh-uair am fuachd ga ghuin.

Mothachaidh gach fear fo 'n ghrèin,
A bhean féin mu 'n dean i chron;
Ma 's bi iad uile gu leir,
Mar tha bhaobh an deigh nan corp.

Seachd righrean chuir i gu leàs,
Thàrladh sud 'na dàil 'us gum b' olc;
Cearaill, 'us Earaill, 'us Fraoch,
'S Cuchullin a sgoilteadh sgiath,
'S Fear Liath an taoibh ghil,
Oissian Mac Shigheigh nan cliar,
Nach diult biadh do neach air bith.

Bha mise an cath an dè,
'S gu 'n robh mi féin an cath cnuic,
An cath callan bho 'n taobh tuath;
'S cath carran bho 'n cruaidh trod.

Is Truisealach mi an dèigh nam Fiann,
'S fada mo phian an deigh chaich;
Air m' ulain 'san aird an iar,
Gu bun mo dhà sgiath an sàs.[11]

Laoidh an Truisealaich

Listen quietly, if you would like a lay
Maiden O, will you guide me?

Great Truiseal, you will have a tale to tell,
Which people were around during your lifetime?
Were you here during the time of the Fenians?
Did you see Fionn, Fial or Fraoch?

Fraoch, son of Cumal of the golden drinking cups,
He was wounded without the protection of weapons;
By the beast of the glen from the north
The son of Cumal fell through hard treachery.

It is a great pity about the pure blood
That was spilt through the deed of the foolish women;

The first day Fraoch went swimming,
As a result of women's voices evil occurred;
He brought his garment to shore,
Mature, smooth, rowan tree without blemish.

That is the flower that I desire,
From the hand of Mac Cumal of the curly hair
Apples from the tree with the highest branches,
That I can see on that loch over there.

Mac Cumal of the drinking cups spoke,
His two cheeks flushed red like blood
He went swimming in a loch on one occasion,
Suffering pain continuously from the cold.

Every man under the sun will suspect,
His own wife before she causes harm;
Before they are all,
Like the wicked woman causing death.

Seven kings she burned to death,
That wicked event happened when she was in their company;
Cearall, Earall, and Fraoch,
And Cuchulainn who would split shields,
And Fear Liath of the white side,
Oissian Mac Shigheigh of the bards,
Who will not refuse food to anyone.

I was in a battle yesterday,
I was in a hill battle,
Against a noisy group from the north;
Battling, trying to escape their hard strife

A Truisealach am I after the Fiann,
Enduring is my pain after the others;
Resting my elbow in the west,
Embedded up to my armpits.

This belief in a sort of enchantment was noted in another form in the mid nineteenth century but perhaps suggesting the ancient owner of the voice:

..many gravely assert that a messenger who proceeded from Ness towards Uig, and who delayed at this spot Contrary to his masters directions, was transformed by him, who was a powerful magician, into the shape of this Stone – And hence say they the name of Clach an Truiseal – Truiseal being a mans name.'[12]

Whatever the mystery and origin of the stone, and however many stories and traditions there are about it, most of the accounts here given have one thing in common apart from their main subject – the need to provide measurements, particularly of height. Few of them seem to agree on this however. At a time when deep peat still surrounded the base of the stone Martin said it was 'above 20 foot high'; about 1790 in similar conditions, with the peat still there, it was 16 feet high, but only a year or two later 18 feet; in 1819 it was back to 16 feet and the same in 1833, but three years later, with the peat removed, it had returned to 18 feet; about 1850 the stone was 'nineteen feet above ground'; then, in 1919 the height was given as 20½ feet, and when the Royal Commission's Inventory of Ancient Monuments volume was published in 1928 the stone's height, measured in 1914, was recorded as 18 feet 10 inches. The variations were probably the outcome of guesswork, perhaps related to the presence and removal of peat, and of repeating figures read in previous descriptions, leaving it open to doubt as to which measurement was the most accurate. Some difference could arise from determining the ground level at the foot of the stone. When measured comparatively recently [September 2006] the height above firm ground was found to be 18 feet 10 inches.

'N uair thigeadh gruaim na h-oidhche teann
Is greann air feadh nam blàr,
'S an driùchd a' sileadh air mo cheann
Tha sealltainn do gach àrd;
Is eoin nan creag air sgiath nan àm,
'N an deann gu'n ionad tàmh,
Gur tric ghabh fasgadh aig mo bhonn
An sprèidh bhiodh trom le h-àl.

Dearcaidh mi bho thaobh mo chùil
Air Mùirneag a' chùil duinn,
Is chì mi ceò gach feasgair ciùin
Ag iadhadh dlùth 's na glinn;
Chì mi bhuam an t-arbhar làn
Air mullach Ard an Tòil;
O, b'eòlach mi air tuar gach àit'
Mus d'thàinig na tha bèo.

Is iomadh neach bha eòlach orm
Tha nise air falbh gu bràth,
Cuid dhiubh cian an grunn na fairg',
'S am Barabhas cuid 'n an tàmh;
'S cuid eile sgapte thall air chuan
Is cuid bha cruaidh 's na blàir,
Gu tric rinn sùgradh ri mo thaobh,
'S air raointean glas na h-Aird.

Clach an Truiseil

When the gloom of the night takes over
And darkens every field
Dew drops fall on my head
That is looking out in every direction;
Sea birds are flying as is their wont,
Swiftly to a place of rest,
Often the herd heavy with their young
Took shelter around my base.

Behind me I can see
Mùirneag of the brown slopes,
And I see mist on every calm evening
Closely surrounding the glens;
I can see beyond the full harvest
On top of Ard an Tòil;
O, I was well acquainted with their appearance
Before those alive today were born.

Many a person who was acquainted with me
Has now departed for ever,
Some are far away at the bottom of the sea,
And some are resting at Barvas;
Others are scattered far across the sea
And some were brave in battle,
Often they played beside me,
On the green fields of the Ard.

Có aig tha fios an ùine a' thriall
'S an cian a tha mi 'n sàs
Bho chunnaic mi air tùs a' ghrian
Cur sgiamh air feadh na h-Aird;
'S a nis ged tha mo ghruag cho liath
A' faicinn triall gach àil,
An so bidh mise gus an tèid
An cruinne-cé 'n a smàl.

The last stanza of this song on Clach an Truiseil, with some variations, was also said to have been derived from 'a Bernera man', perhaps around 1960 or earlier [D Macdonald (coll.): Tales and Traditions of the Lews Stornoway 1967 p.102]:

Co aig tha fhios an ùin a thriall,
'S an cian tha mi 's àn aite-sa?
Bho chunna mi air tùs a' ghrian
Cur sgiamh air feur nam blàth
A nis ged tha mo cheann cho liath,
'S mi faicinn triall gach àl;
An so bidh' mise gus an téid
An cruinne-cé 'na smàl.'

Clach an Truiseil

Who knows the years that have passed
Since I first stood here
Since I first saw the sun
Enhancing the beauty of the Àrd;
And now although my head has greyed
Watching the generations pass by,
Here I will be
Until the earth is consumed by fire.

Who knows the time that has passed,
And the years I have been here?
Since I first saw the sun
Enhancing the beauty of the flowers and plants
Now though my head is grey,
And I watch the generations pass;
Here I will be
Until the earth is consumed by fire.

References and Notes

1. Royal Commission on Ancient and Historical Monuments and Constructions of Scotland – Ninth Report with Inventory of Monuments and Constructions in the Outer Hebrides, Skye and the Small Isles Edinburgh 1928 p.7 no.16, pp.7-8 no.17; M Martin: A Description of the Western Islands of Scotland London 1703 pp.8-9
2. OSNB – microfilm copy in Western Isles Libraries, Stornoway
3. C Mackenzie: 'An Account of some Remains of Antiquity in the Island of Lewis, one of the Hebrides' in Archaeologia Scotica Vol.I p.285
4. The Statistical Account of Scotland Reprint Wakefield 1983 Vol.XX The Western Isles (Parish of Barvas) p.9
5. W Daniell: A Voyage round the north and north-west Coast of Scotland and the Adjacent Islands London n.d
6. A V Seaton (edit.): Journal of an Expedition to the Feroe and Westman Islands and Iceland 1835 by George Clayton Atkinson Newcastle upon Tyne 1989 p.45
7. The New Statistical Account of Scotland Edinburgh & London 1845 – Ross & Cromarty (parish of Barvas) pp.145-146
8. N Macdonald (edit.): The Morrison Manuscript – Traditions of the Western Isles by Donald Morrison, Cooper, Stornoway Stornoway 1975 p.22. The site of 'Knockruagan' is on the opposite side of the Grimersta river from Linshader. Other versions of the story give Brue and Arnol as alternative battle sites. W Matheson: 'MacAulays – Second Series' in Stornoway Gazette 26 February 1957. The 'clan battle' tale seems to have been believed by W Anderson Smith in Lewsiana London 1875 p.179: 'a large menhir near Barvas was erected in historic times by the Morrisons of Ness, a Scandinavian race, to commemorate a victory over the Macaulays of Uig: it is larger than the centre stone of Callernish'. The Macaulays were most probably 'a Scandinavian race', while the Morrisons may originally have derived from Ireland

9   W C Mackenzie: <u>History of the Outer Hebrides</u> Paisley 1903 p.64; W C Mackenzie: <u>The Book of the Lews</u> Paisley 1919 pp.223-224

10 D Macdonald: <u>Lewis – A History of the Island</u> Edinburgh 1978 p.14. Murdo Morrison (Murchadh a' Bhocs), of Shader, Barvas, composed a song about Clach an Truiseil, possibly around 1922 [M Morrison: <u>Fear Siubhal nan Gleann – Orain agus Dain</u> Glasgow (1923 ?) pp.33-35]

11 An introductory note was added by the editor (Campbell): 'This is an imaginary conversation with a great standing Stone in the Ness of Lewis, in the Parish of Barras. It is curious because made up of names, and of single lines of Ballads which are recited entire in the neighbouring Islands ... Murray, the reciter, asserts that it was the custom in his youth to recite this "Lay of the Truiseal Stone," near the butt of Lewis in Shawbost.' The township of Shawbost was possibly named because Macphail, not Murray, came from that place

12 <u>Ordnance Survey Name Book</u> – see n.2 above

stone axes and other implements, a defensive island retreat in a moorland loch, possibly even boundary marks and the ingredients of a language, all for the future to find accidentally or deliberately. A person exploring the island today, or even that small part of it between Tolsta and Ness, can consider these things in the course of a walk or while resting on a convenient, sun-warmed stone.

The Norsemen arrived around 800 A.D. and gave this place, whatever might have been its former name, their own title, the earliest to have survived until the present day. This was *Tolsta*, signifying originally 'Tholf's farmstead', the possession of a leading figure for whom it was a source of income and status. The amount of land he held may well have been measured in 'pennylands', whatever they may be, and have been in total 'the ten pennylands of Tolestaff [Tolsta]' recorded in 1590, comparable with 'the five pennylands of Borve' or 'the Seven penny lands of Shader'.

So now we can picture an individual or group of people coming to this place in the mid 1850s and wondering about its past, its name and origin, about the very first folk who settled here. In a sense an expedition from Tolsta to Ness in 1855 could begin far back in time, with the state of the landscape itself and the traces of early human occupation many centuries ago. In the time of the early Norsemen Tolsta was a single unit, inhabited by its principal resident and an unknown number of other less important but nevertheless useful retainers, who could be called upon to give armed support in time of need but usually served as workers of the land and crews of boats. At some point, perhaps after that Norse presence had faded and been followed by people of mixed Norse and Celtic blood, the chapel of St Michael in 'Tollasta' was built as a place where people of the early Christian faith could seek religious comfort; and in addition to the name of 'Tolsta' itself words or parts of words of Norse origin mixed with Gaelic and remained in use among the place-names and the language of the area, identifying features along the coast and well inland, for instance 'Gil', 'Giordale', 'Earrascro', 'Lingavat' and probably 'Muirneag'. The location of the ancient Tolsta settlement is not certainly known, but it may have been on the good land at or near the point afterwards called Seann Bhaile (the old town), not far from the shore and close to the probable site of the St Michael chapel, at 'Cladh Mhicheil', the old burial ground.

Two Tolstas and the Macivers

It is unlikely that anyone heading for Ness around 1855, or today, would have brought along a copy of one of the oldest maps of Lewis, the one probably surveyed in the 1590s and none too accurate as a record of the island's shape. Indeed it would have been unwise to carry through the moor such a valuable item, which would be best studied indoors at home. But that map has the name of 'Tollosta' correctly situated northwards from Gress and Back, and with a long stretch of bare-looking coast continuing up towards the settlement of 'Sgiogarstagh' in Ness. By the time the map was published in 1654 it may be that the ancient settlement at Tolsta deserved more than a single name, because either in previous years or in years soon to come there was a division of the settlement into two parts, South and North Tolsta, each of which included a cluster or 'town' (baile) of houses, outbuildings and some of the pennylands. The boundary between the two seems to have run beside a stream called Allt Chaluim Chille, St Columba's stream, at the mouth of which it ran into the long strand known as the 'Tràigh Mhòr'. This stream could be traced up the hill to its source in the moor behind the settlements. The name of the stream alone heightens the sense of antiquity which accompanies the vicinity of Seann Bhaile.[2]

Eventually other written records came into being, knowledge of which would have been a useful companion on the way north. There is for instance the rental of the forfeited Seaforth Estate of Lewis in 1718, which contained the following entry and showed that at both South and North Tolsta walkers to Ness in that early year, as in the 1850s, were in Maciver country:

'Alexr. Mckiver in North Tolsta for himself and for Rory Mckiver in South Tolsta his son Makes oath That he and his Son pay each of them for their possession of the said Lands of North and South Tolstas, One hundred and thirteen punds Seventeen shilling four pennies, One boll meall Six Mutten, and three stones butter, and no more and that he is in no arrear having payed the former rents to the Chamberlain Which is the truth as he shall answer to God.'[3]

The two Macivers, father and son, were still in possession of the same farms or 'tacks' eight years later in 1726, and the close relationship within one family may indicate that South and North Tolsta were already being run together as a single holding once more.[4] Over the next 25 or 27 years the younger Maciver, Roderick, otherwise Rory, held both farms himself and was undoubtedly one of the principal tacksmen in Lewis.

But towards the end of this period things began to change. On 20 August 1754 'Roderick McEiver' (Rory) once again took the single tack of the 'Two Tolstays' for another twelve years, and two local tenants gave evidence as to the manner in which land there was held from the tacksman, who in turn held the whole from the proprietor, Mackenzie of Seaforth. First of all, 'Donald McNeil Tenent in South Tolstay', a married man aged 55, was asked what rent 'South Tolstay' paid to Roderick Maciver and he answered as follows:

'That the town of South Tolstay Consists of Six penies of Land which is possesst by Sixteen tenents That he the Deponent possesses an half penie which pays yearly of Money Rent one pound ten Shilings Six pence and two thirds of a penie So that the whole Town pays Eighteen pound Six Shilings and eight pence Sterling Money Rent Depons that the Sixteen tenents possessing South Tolstay pays a weekly days Service a Cock and hen a peck of Meal and a Coil of heather rops yearly and that each half penie pays 2 Shilings and Six pence Dry Multures yearly Depons that he the Deponent and the other fifteen Tenents possessing South Tolstay Agreed to give the said Roderick McEiver Tacksman fifty Merks Scots in name of Grassum for each half penie of South Tolstay for twelve years L[e]ase further Depons that the town of North Tolstay Consist of Six penies land and is possesst by the Tacksman that when it was possesst by Tenents it payed the Same Rent with Sowth Tolstay but that now it is much abused by Sand Drift and not so good as South Tolstay ...'

The latter remarks on North Tolsta are of interest here. It seems likely that the 'Sand Drift' was the result of some easterly or northerly gales, and that therefore the land worked by tenants was damaged to the extent that the tenants may have been forced to move. It is not clear where they moved to, if they did move, but they might have found space in South Tolsta or migrated further afield, some of them perhaps even to Ness.

Following the deposition of Donald Macneil another occupant of 'South Tolstay' gave evidence. This was 'Malcom McInish Tenent in South Tolstay', also a married man and aged 46. On being 'examined as to what rent the Tenents pay to the said Tacks[man]' he confirmed what Macneil had said 'with respect to the yearly payments and Entrie of South and North Tolstays', and he stated that he had lived in 'Tolstay' for the past seventeen years

Chapter III

– no doubt wishing to show that he knew what he was talking about.

When the twelve years were up and the tack was at an end the two Tolstas nearly disappeared from the record – but not quite. The next rental, of 1766, had no entries for South and North Tolsta, but there were still two references to 'Tolsta', of an entirely different kind. They introduced an official connection with Ness for the first time. One ran as follows:

'Compeared Donald Roy, Donald Pipper, John MacAlister, Donald McEon, Donald McInnes, Malcom McCoilvi[e or c?], and Norman Gillyriach who agree to take the farm of Knockard [in Ness] with a proportion of the hill of Tolsta at the yearly rent of Twenty seven pounds four shillings and two pence Sterling ..'

The sum paid as rent, £27.4s.2d, was the same as that paid by ten tenants for their lands of Fivepenny Ness in 1766, without the additional hill land, so it could have been that the 'Knockard' tenants were allowed part of the Tolsta grazing for nothing. But that is not certain. The other reference to Tolsta was similar to the first:

'Compeared Donald McCoil, John McCoil, John McEonvicfinlay, John McEonvicCoil, Donald Mchorimat, John Mccoilroy, Donald McEoncuil, John McWilliam, Donald McEon, Kent. MacEon, Alexr. More, Malcom Garve, Angus McLeod, John McGillyrevach, Donald Morison, Donald McEonvicCoil, Angus Bain, Angus Morison, Murdo McEon, and Donald Bain who agree to take the farm of Europee [in Ness] deducing therefrom the pendicle of Skegersta and adding in place thereof a part of the hill grass of Tolsta at the yearly rent of Thirty One pounds eight shillings Str. including therein five bolls farm meal ..'

This rental thus gave twenty seven tenants in the north of Ness rights to pasture stock on land associated with Tolsta. Perhaps they were also allowed to build shieling shelters in that hill area, though it is not made clear what the boundaries of the area were, nor why the Ness people were permitted use of it.[5]

❖

The arrangement under which the tenants of 'Eòropaidh' and 'Knockard' were entitled to use the hill pastures of Tolsta was probably a temporary one. The rental of 1780, when lands were let for seven years, shows that 'John Mac Eiver Junior Shipmaster in Stornoway' agreed to accept once again his existing possession of 'South and North Tolstays' at the annual rent of £36 sterling, and, seven years later, the same situation was renewed at the increased price of £42.

There was no further mention of Ness involvement either in the 1780s or thereafter, but of course there were many other forms of connection between the two districts, perhaps mainly social rather than agricultural. As marriages between Tolsta and Ness families increased, kinship became an ever more important link, with the visiting and lodging of relatives which went along with it. In summer, going to the shielings in the moor provided an opportunity for occupants from Tolsta and Ness townships to mix with each other, and for ceilidhs and courtships. In due course Ness people walked to Tolsta and Back in order to attend communions, and the reverse could happen as well according to the season. Finding and collecting stray stock also meant exchange of hospitality. In 1914 five of the six Tolsta fishing boats were 'sgoth' built in Ness, and there may have been nothing new in that. No doubt for good reason the associations and relationships joining one area to the other were more abundant than a stranger would guess.

Venturing northwards from the two Tolstas soon led a walker of earlier days to realise that any boundary distinguishing Tolsta at the high cliffs of Lighe nan Leac, this time a mile north of Dùn Othail.

In this way Dùn Othail, which had formerly been north of the boundary of North Tolsta, fell within the area of Tolsta Farm and so, for a while, was felt to belong as much to Tolsta as it did to Ness. There were few places along the walk to Sgiogarstagh as significantly interesting as Dùn Othail and therefore at best its value as a striking attraction to visitors and to those Ness and Tolsta people who were concerned with their historical and traditional past could, at this stage, be shared.

The introduction of Tolsta Farm did not only call into question the association of Dùn Othail with two distinct areas. It also invented a new northern boundary, taking a small part of Ness into a land unit which chiefly belonged to the world of Tolsta. It might well be asked why this happened, particularly as it ignored the long-established parish boundary which was clearly entered on the map of Lewis published in 1822.

The parishes involved in 1822 were those of Ness and Stornoway, and the relevant stretch of boundary line was shown on the map of that date as running from a point on the coast somewhere near Dùn Othail out to a loch named 'Loch Murnaick', north-east of the hill known as Mùirneag. The Stornoway side of this line was coloured pink, the Ness side yellow, and at the loch it met the parish of Barvas for which the colour was green. By the time of the Ordnance Survey's presence around 1851-52 the name 'Loch Murnaick' had disappeared, as had the colours, and the boundary had been clarified by the more accurate definition of the landscape and the introduction of many place-names. The line between the parishes, beginning at Geodh' a Ghille, just north of Callaige, ran straight south-west, no doubt taking the same route as the less exact coloured boundary of 1822. Its starting point was on the sea cliffs, and its course was now marked by a series of deliberately created mounds, the last of which to be noted here was that on Beinn nan Caorach already mentioned. Walkers going north from Tolsta thus entered Ness parish and district by crossing the line of mounds, and Tolsta Farm included a part of Ness because its northern boundary curved over that line and did so only two or three years after the mounds were established.

Setting out for Ness

Many people must have walked between Tolsta and Ness, one way or the other, in the days before Tolsta Farm came into existence. It is highly likely that, generation after generation, they followed a familiar route which had become visible over the rough terrain through being worn by innumerable footsteps. But the first person to walk there and to be recorded by name in print was probably Thomas S. Muir, who wrote a brief sketch about crossing that part of the moorland.

Muir, who was a keen student of ancient churches, chapels, duns and brochs, first visited Lewis in 1857. He began by going one day to Tolsta, mainly, it seems, because, on the way, he wanted to see 'the church of St Aula' at Gress, the ruin of which still stands close to the road and is therefore easily noticed without having to make a lengthy expedition. 'Farther on in the same direction,' he wrote, 'we come next upon the long blackened homestead of Tolsta, overhanging a lengthened curve of smooth sandy beach – the *traigh mhor* of the Ordnance map – between its towering headland, and the wild moorland track with its high rugged coastline extending to the fishing port of Ness at the Butt of Lewis.' By 'track' he probably meant 'tract', the stretch of moor he could see ahead of him, and he chose not to go much further on that day. Why had he called Tolsta a 'blackened homestead'? Was that a way of describing the recently and forcibly abandoned homes of North Tolsta?

Muir next crossed over to the west side of the island to see the sights there, and then moved north by Barvas, Borve and Cross to Port of Ness where he lodged with Kenneth Murray (Coinneach Gobha) and his wife at 'Tota Gormaig'. He visited Rona and Sulasgeir, picked up local knowledge about those islands and some of the Ness monuments, then completed his initial journey to Tolsta by going south from Port and Sgiogarstagh. His comments on this latter part of his route were addressed to an imaginary visitor of the future:

'should you desire to see something of the moorland life and scenery of northern Lewis, your plan will be to take your return to Stornoway along the eastern side of the island. As there is, however, for the greater part of the journey, no guidance more than the often not very discernible tracings of a projected road, or drift-way, broken up every here and there by wild ruts and water-courses, the route will be found rather a dull and toilsome one, except in fine weather.'

In recommending this manner of leaving Ness for Stornoway Thomas Muir was of course seeing the walk from, as it were, the opposite end of our already imagined expedition. But what was of particular interest in Muir's description was his reference to the irregular presence of 'a projected road', just visible enough in places to serve as a guide to those venturing into the wilds. The word 'projected' suggests that at some point in the not very remote past someone had planned to make a road sufficient for the passage of carts and even carriages between Tolsta and Ness. The initiator of the undertaking was most probably the proprietor of Lewis, James Matheson, or his factor, and by the time of Muir's visit it appears that while for some of the way this plan had only been implemented to the extent of perhaps digging ditches, heaping up rows of peat and turf, or setting down preliminary lines of track, a start had been made on more definite construction at the north and south ends. Matheson's factor in 1851, John Munro Mackenzie, himself investigated the undertaking on Saturday 16 August that year and recorded the fact in his diary:

'Walked over the line of proposed road between Ness and Tolsta, there are nearly 100 men at present at work on this road at the Ness end – They are paid at the rate of 1s per yard of finished roadway one half in Destitution Meal and the other half Credited in their rents – Let several sections of the road to Contractors and placed McMillan (who superintended the Uig Road) as foreman between Ness and Tolsta – The Tolsta people are by no means so keen for the work as the Ness men, and it is ill to get them to do any work.'[6]

The detailed Ordnance map surveyed in 1852 and to which Muir, and Mackenzie, referred, showed that the waving 'road' or track from Stornoway that touched upon Gress and then South and North Tolsta already continued on north over several of the streams as far as a point in the moor just across Feadan Nighean a' Bhreitheimh, which runs out of the south tip of Loch Caol Dhùin Othail. At this stage the road disappeared from the map, then reappeared more than a mile further on and just to the east of Loch Sgeireach na Creige Briste, stopped again for a short distance, but resumed at Gil an Tairbh and then ran all the way to Lìonal without a break.[7]

It was not difficult for walkers of the 1850s to pick up this route on setting out through Tolsta Farm and to note the sources of road-making material. As they left the house sites of old North Tolsta they might have noticed three of the seven mills on Allt na Muilne, just beside the road, and from there on round Beinn Gheireadha and Creag Mhòr there was a sequence of gravel pits, often only a few yards apart, out of which had no doubt come the foundations and surface of the new road in that area. In all probability that part of the road must therefore have been finished or nearly finished not long before. There was a pause in the pit series at Amhuinn Gheireadha and Allt na Cloich where the road passed through the racing water, although each river crossing, which could be difficult and even dangerous in wet weather, was accompanied on the map by 'Proposed Bridge'. The gravel pits thereafter became fewer, until they were non-existent, an indication that construction work had not yet reached that point.

Road-making to connect significant locations with Stornoway had begun in the time of Matheson's predecessor, Stewart Mackenzie, and by 1820 a highway existed across the moor to Barvas. It did not however extend all the way to the Ness townships for several more years, but it would have struck any landowner that it would be preferable to establish a link through Shader, Borve and Galson to the developing fishery harbour at the new village of Port of Ness rather than take the more or less uninhabited way from Tolsta to Ness. However, it might also have occurred to either Stewart Mackenzie or Matheson that the gap between Tolsta and Ness was narrow enough to be worth closing with a road connection, but this idea might rather have appealed to the financially well-off Matheson than to the impoverished landowner who in 1844 sold him the estate. For some reason, though, work on the road seems to have stopped shortly before Muir tried to follow it, and his attention was drawn towards the various antiquities that he could see to one side.

A Walk from Tolsta to Ness in the 1850s

Caisteal a' Mhorair, Tràigh Geiraha a short way north of Tolsta

ground dotted with half a dozen small ruined buildings. But having done so and felt some frustration at being so near Dùn Othail and yet so far from it, those hopeful visitors had to move on, whether to north or south, and content themselves in future with recollection of the traditional tales told about this dramatic place.[9]

And so, turning away from Dùn Othail, walkers going north picked up the road again, such as it was, where it skirted Loch Sgeireach and approached the south end of Loch Caol Dùin Othail. Here, as already explained and at one stride over Feadan Nighean a' Bhreitheamh, they put the land of Tolsta Farm behind them and entered at last unmistakably Ness ground. But almost at the same moment they lost the road which, since it bent up the slope from Amhuinn na Cloich, had been not much more than a preliminary outline through the soft, uneven boggy ground and now stopped altogether. Thereafter they had an open stretch of a little more than a mile to the east side of Loch Sgeireach na Creige Briste, where suddenly the road, or its outline, started again and ran on for about half a mile, aiming for Dìbadal. Why, they probably wondered, had it been given up for that mile or so, and, indeed, why was it not yet being brought to a finished condition all the way?

If, along that trackless stretch, they strayed nearer to the cliffs they would have found better, drier ground to walk on, and would have enjoyed the coastal views as they went along, though of course they would not have been able to see the caves formed by the attacks of the sea down below. On the other hand, if they had wandered off in the opposite direction into the great, open moor, they would have been surrounded by a company of large and small lochs, a mass of pools and spongy wet land, frequented by lonely-looking birds, red-throated divers, snipe and dunlin, but rarely disturbed by any other human presence except in the summer when people came to the shielings at Geàrraidh Bhat a Leòis, beside Loch Bhat a Leòis where they could collect the valued plant known as 'lus na laoigh'.[10]

As often happens, anyone whose attention is taken up by the advantageous route near the cliff edges generally misses noticing the shieling huts at the north end of Loch Caol Dhùin Othail and is even less likely to see those at Geàrraidh Loch Eilleagbhal, a little further to the west, where there were some already long forsaken. On the other hand, in the 1850s, and probably in the better days of early summer when the ground was comparatively dry, it was not unusual for a lonely wayfarer here to meet an occupant of a shieling out with cattle, or to sniff the scent of peat smoke, or to come across a 'gearraidh' and spend an hour in interesting talk. But assuming that that person concentrated on the cliff route and went past Loch Sgeireach na Creige Briste, with the four abandoned and ruined summer dwellings on its western shore, eyes fixed either on the turf in front of already wet feet or on a fishing boat out at sea, the sudden appearance of an unexpected house provided a shock. This building stood on hard, green ground, from which stones for the walls had been cut, and was very much alone high above the sea. It was surrounded only by the soft, varied colours of the moor. The name of the place was Cùilatotair, and the neglected roof and walls evoked family memories among the descendants of Macdonalds and Macleods who had lived there in the 1820s and 1830s after having each resided for periods of about five years on the island of Rona. Quite why they should have gone to the wilds of Cùilatotair on leaving Rona remains something of a mystery.

Leaving Cùilatotair behind and going directly west the last part of the half-mile piece of road was reached, and then it

Chapter III

almost immediately disappeared again. Not far in front were the two main streams of Dìbadal. The first, Gil an Tairbh, emerged from Loch Langabhat, the largest loch in northern Lewis, and ran more quickly down the slope to converge with the second, Gil Dhìbadail, in a deep gully opening to the sea at a stony shore. Jutting from this shore rocks ended in Eilean Glas Cùilatotair, a tiny lump of an island whose name related it across Dìbadal to the house already encountered. The lower part of Gil an Tairbh above the confluence of the streams was gloomily bordered by lines of rocky crags, which meant that the road, which started again on the south side of Gil an Tairbh, crossed the stream at a higher level and maintained height until it met Gil Dhìbadail, where it passed close by the three houses of Dìbadal Uarach and straightened on a gentle slope to head directly north. A turn to the left here would lead at the same height along the heathery slope to Dìbadal Iorach, two groups each of two or three buildings which looked down on a few huts at the mouth of the Dìbadal 'river', two hundred and fifty feet below.[11]

Thomas Muir, with his own versions of Gaelic spellings, came to Dìbadal probably from Lional and found it a pleasant place. He may have seen an eagle or two here as he walked around the deep little glen:

'At Dhìbadail – a small fine grassy spot on the slopes of a deep dell, threaded by a rivulet more bright and volant than the thrave [majority] of Lewis rivers – you will be amused with the shealings of the Lionol and Habost crofters, who are over to summer their cows upon the fresh moorland pasture, whilst the home grazings are being recruited and economised for autumn and winter use.'

He then described shieling life as he saw it:
'One of the younger and stouter females out of each family,

wealthy enough to own a few kine, is generally the person who is sent across on this lonely service, accompanied, however, by one or two of the children to help her, and look after the bothy during her occasional journeys either to her home, or to some trysting-place midway, with the produce of the dairy. The size of the shealing varies a good deal. Sometimes its interior does not exceed 7 or 8 feet square; sometimes, when the animals are housed in it, which is oftener the case than not, the length of the building is considerable: but whether short or long, the slightly elevated portion allotted to the human occupants is just roomy enough to quarter the narrow stone-fenced bed on the ground, the central hearth, and the two or three trifling articles forming the cooking and churning apparatus of the rude household.'

This glimpse of Dìbadal suggests that the buildings in the little groups on the side of the hill above Gil Dhìbadail were all shielings, which they were indeed then and afterwards, used by people from Habost and Lìonal. But it is possible that at one time one or two of them were permanently occupied, as was Cùilatotair. It is time, however, to leave them behind, or, more exactly, to leave Dìbadal Iorach and decide whether to return to the road or go on by the cliff tops leading to Seileir (Cellar Head).

Maoim and Cuidhaseadair

In spite of Muir's remark that the 'sgeirs, stacs, and land-rocks along the shore, on which you occasionally find yourself, are frequently on a gigantic scale, and of singular configuration', 1850s visitors, without going to see for themselves, would have concluded that Muir was also right in saying that 'there is little to arouse attention' along this part of the coast, and so they would rejoin the road which was a little more distinct than it had been. This new grass etc.' These last remarks would apply to many of the shielings in the Ness district and elsewhere.[15]

At the next stream, a branch of Allt Chasgro, but well up the slope of Campar Mòr, were Airidhean nan Grùigean, a 'number of Shealings, Some of which are in ruins'. Like those by Allt Chasgro they were 'built of peat-moss and Stone' and were 'very large', being used in the early part of the Summer for housing Sheep and Cattle'. It seemed that no sooner was this point left than a third group of dwellings was at hand, Airidh nan Geàrraidhean, a name which suggests more than one enclosure or arable area. The road ran straight through the middle of the group, so perhaps there was a 'gearraidh' on each side. Certainly the buildings were. They were large, built of peat moss and stone, and mostly in ruins, though two on the right hand side were still complete with heather and peat moss thatch. The water supply here was the first of three tributaries that joined to make Amhuinn Chaithaseadair, which enjoyed only a short life before it entered the sea. This name was derived from a small and old settlement called Caithaseadair, up the slope north of the river, to which the surveyors of 1852 referred as 'The ruins of a few old houses which were occupied about 50 years ago, by one family' and which 'Scarcely can be seen'. A small patch of arable land surrounded them. As another 'seadair' this place was probably again of great antiquity.

Almost certainly the 'one family' known to have lived at Caithaseadair had been that of Angus Maclean, called by his local Gaelic name of Aonghas Mòr Riabhach. He and a brother came from Harris and made their home at Caithaseadair, where, so the story goes, 'they enclosed enough ground to produce winter feed for their cattle'. They lived there for several years, but then the brother married and settled in the township of Bragar some distance away. Angus, on the other hand, married a lady from

'Knockard', Margaret Macdonald, and became a tenant under the 1814 lotting of that place with his house on a site known as No.5. The area north of the house site was later remembered as 'Iodhlainn Aonghais Riabhaich'. Though he made this move Angus continued to graze cattle at Caithaseadair until 1829 and possibly afterwards. According to a later story what were believed to be pirate ships fired canon balls that landed on the settlement and one or two of these were subsequently found and kept at a house in Adabroc or Eorodale. A further feature of this interesting area visible to someone passing along the road, had it been known they were there, was a number of small mounds identified as graves situated between Caithaseadair and the sea cliffs. They were supposed to contain the remains of people from a sailing vessel wrecked on the rocks of the nearby shore.

It happened that the name 'Caithaseadair' could be easily confused with 'Cuidhaseadair', and the two had always to be carefully distinguished from one another.

Not far north of the third of the Amhuinn Chaithaseadair tributaries, Allt a Mhaide, the settlements of Sgiogarstagh came fully into sight. These were a possible conclusion to the walk from Tolsta, and to reach them it was necessary to turn off the road in the direction of the sea. But before this could be done two further groups of shieling huts, Seilastotair and Bhata Guaille, had to be passed; both of them were situated on the bank of Allt Sheilastotair just upstream from the road. The nearer, Seilastotair, consisted of several dwellings, about six, all close together yet 'of a larger size than the generality of Shealings in the Lewis', and 'used in the early part of the Summer Season for housing Cattle etc'. Perhaps it was owing to their position close to the road and to a sand pit that they were very much in a habitable state. There was also a story about Seilastotair which began by

Chapter III

9   For traditions concerning Dùn Othail – M Robson: <u>Forts and Fallen Walls – The duns of northern Lewis</u> Port of Ness 2004 pp.21-23, 33-34. The Ordnance Survey maps of the area, surveyed in 1852 and published two years later, showed a ruined building on the south-east shoulder of Dùn Othail, so at least one of the surveyors must have gone ashore and climbed up

10 Presumably the same as 'Lus-nan-laogh' (Golden Saxifrage – according to Dwelly's dictionary p.617)

11 In addition to its extent Loch Langabhat was 'said to abound in black trout of a considerable size'; and a 'considerable portion of its water is drawn off by a drain into Amhuinn Dhail, for the purpose of working the 'Dhail Corn-mill'

12 OSNB 146 The surveyors' description of 'Maoim' was: 'Several shealings on both sides of Feadan na Maoim, some of which are in ruins: the remainder are occupied by people from Tabost' [i.e. Habost]

13 OSNB 146. The surveyors' comment on 'Dun Bhilascleiter' was: 'There is a small ruin of an oblong form, on its Summit, from which, perhaps, the name has been derived. There is no part of the walls standing, but the stones of which it was composed are large and tolerably regular'

14 Census Return 1851. The four 'Out House' lodgers were William McDonald [born in Thurso parish], Donald McDonald [born in Stornoway parish], Allan McDeirmed [widower aged 30, born in Harris parish], George McAulay [born in Uig parish, Lewis]

15 OSNB 145

16 Paper read at a meeting of the Lewis Branch of the E.I.S. on Saturday, 7 November [1903] by Mr Mackenzie, Shader. [CWC No.85 Lewis Place-names]

17 The contents of this Postscript are taken from records [e.g. NRS AF67/269] noted by Donald Macdonald in preparing his book on the Tolsta townships [see n.2 above]

Chapter IV
Dòmhnull Cam

One of the many streams that rise among the hills of south-east Lewis and, after a few miles of rough moorland, disappear into Loch Seaforth is known as Allt Airidh Dhòmhnuill Chaim. The numerous springs of its tributaries are mostly up on the broad west flank of Sìthean an Airgid; and these small, often scarcely visible trickles increase in size a little as they descend until they meet below, just east of the prominent, rocky but not very high hill called Cithis Bheag. Here the uniting waters bend towards the north and run on down into the stony shore of the sea loch.

Only a few yards before it joins the loch the stream passes through a group of three ruined buildings, one at least of which seems to have given its name to the 'Allt', for the ruined walls near its right bank, or in fact all three on both sides, are said to be the visible remains of Airidh Dhòmhnuill Chaim, the shieling of Dòmhnull Cam.

There are, however, some problems associated with the name and with the buildings themselves. Dòmhnull Cam, as will be seen, was a Macaulay whose home country was far away to the west in the district of Uig on the opposite side of the island, and with so much wild land on his own doorstep available for shielings it is difficult to imagine why he should have come so many miles for such a purpose. Nevertheless it is of interest that the place-name exists and that it was recorded at least as early as 1852, by which time there seems to have been a connection between the district hemmed in by Loch Seaforth, the Minch and Loch Shell, and the people of Uig. On the coast near the mouth of Loch Shell

Chapter IV

Stac Dhòmhnuill Chaim

simple shelter like a shieling hut in which a man might lodge almost with comfort:

'It extends for about thirty yards in an Easterly direction from high water mark. There is a small aperture at its end which is just large enough to admit of air and no more. There is no possibility of getting into it as its mouth is always closed by each succeeding swell of the sea, and which causes a great noise at the aperture above mentioned.'

Such an inhospitable recess, nearly always inaccessible and filled with sea surge except perhaps at the innermost end, was not a pleasant place. It was known as Prìosan Dhòmhnuill Chaim, Dòmhnull Cam's Prison.

Two questions arise. Was he an occasional captive here, or was the cave also a refuge where he hid from pursuit? But the real question, requiring an answer before either of these two can be asked, is, could he or anyone else get into the cave and survive? If not, then the rest of conjecture about Dòmhnull Cam's presence here is a matter of whether to accept what would seem to be a fairly insubstantial tradition, again, as with the nature and purpose of Airidh Dhòmhnuill Chaim, perhaps no more than a piece of imagination and local humour.

❖

However unlikely it might appear to be that the cave could be used as a retreat and place of hiding, it is necessary to have in mind that there is a third, and certainly the most distinguished and famed, coastal haunt associated with Dòmhnull Cam, this one being in his own home country of Uig. It is today a rocky tower among the cliffs at Mangursta, very nearly inaccessible and therefore extremely difficult to explore. This natural tower is commonly called Stac Dhòmhnuill Chaim.

on the summit of the Stac and reported on their condition. They found severe erosion taking place and concluded as follows:

'The archaeological remains on Stac Dhomhnuill Chaim are in the process of being rapidly eroded. It is possible that, depending on winter storm conditions, the next two decades may see the total destruction of the site. It will soon become effectively inaccessible.'

So they recommended that the site be 'totally excavated, as a matter of urgency, within the next five years'. The five years are now in the past, and excavation has not yet taken place.

The Stac itself is still joined to 'mainland' Lewis by a narrow ridge, but to descend to this ridge and to ascend from it to the Stac site is becoming an increasingly difficult and dangerous task, and the large and very loose rocks add to the risky nature of walking along the ridge. What Thomas mentioned as a path is now scarcely visible and does not in the least provide a clear route up the Stac.

Two small structures were shown on the summit of the Stac in 1852-53, but they were accompanied by no name and no indication of function. When visited in 2004 three small 'buildings' were examined. One was a perimeter wall of stone and turf, extending from the northern or ridge end of the Stac along the eastern side and at its southern end it became 'harder to define, but possibly encloses two terraces'. On the upper terrace are the remains of the other buildings, while at the southern end of the second or lower terrace 'occasional masonry' is an indication of a possibly earlier wall, perhaps representing an older and longer perimeter enclosure. A 'circular turf and stone building adjoining the perimeter wall' at the north-eastern edge of the Stac appeared to have no entrance, and neither did a roughly rectangular building of the same material in the centre of the summit space. In the absence of excavation there is 'no concrete evidence' of the site's 'date range' or purpose, but the discovery of two pieces of pottery that might have been made locally at any time between a distant, prehistoric period and the twentieth century may indicate occupation of the Stac many centuries ago.[3]

❖

As for the story of Dòmhnull Cam Macaulay himself most of what is known about him derives from tradition, but, as pointed out by Captain F W L Thomas and by William Matheson, there are two historical records of him. One comes in 1605 and is a significant part of what is known about his family. The other, dated five years later, records how the Scottish Privy Council, on hearing that the fugitive Dòmhnull Cam and a probably related companion called Mulcallum McCoul had found shelter at Dunvegan Castle in Skye, issued a warrant dated 24th July 1610 ordaining and commanding Rory Mòr Macleod, laird at Dunvegan, 'to detene and keip Donald Cam McCoull and Mulcallum McCoul, who are presentlie in his custodie and keeping, until the last of Maii nixttocum, which is the dyet appointit for the said Donaldis compeirance before the saidis Lordis'. It has been assumed that Dòmhnull Cam never appeared before the Privy Council, and in 1614 Rory Mòr was in ward in Edinburgh Castle 'for not exhibitione of some of the rebellis of the Lewis.'[4]

The many tales told about Dòmhnull Cam and the family of Macaulays to which he belonged were fortunately gathered together from tradition by a certain Donald Morrison, cooper in Stornoway, whose collection was considered by Thomas as 'the foundation' of nearly all subsequently published versions. These traditions were written by Morrison in nine notebooks, of which two have been considered lost for well over a hundred years. Captain Thomas's account of Morrison and his work is probably as near to a short biography as surviving information will allow. Who was this Donald Morrison?

'Donald Morrison, although of Lewis descent, was a Harris man by birth, for he was born in May 1787, at Dirishgill (i.e., Deers-gil), on the south side of Loch Resort, in the wildest part of a wild country. The place is full of high mountains and deep glens, and when Torran [Taran] Mor is angry the winds roar and howl and hiss, and the sea is white with whirling foam, and the surface of the river-like loch is like a battlefield for mist and tumult. But the boy was soon removed to Errista, Uig, and was afterwards a schoolmaster for five years at Valtos. He then went to Stornoway, and was a shopman with Mr Murdo Macleod, cooper and shipowner. He afterwards commenced business on his own account, failed, and then followed the trade of a cooper. About this time he began, on his own suggestion, to write his "Traditions," in which he was encouraged by the late Rev. W Macrae, Barvas, and the Rev. J Cameron, Stornoway.'

'Although a Morrison by name he was brought up in the country of the Macaulays, which accounts for the greater fullness and reality of his traditions concerning them. Most of this lore he obtained from his stepfather, who was well-versed in the legends of that place.

'Donald Morrison married in 1810, had twelve children, and died in August 1824. He was three years writing his books, writing and taking notes from people, with no other desk than a board across his knees.'

Thomas also noted that in Uig Donald Morrison was known as 'Domhnull Ban Sgoilear, i.e., Donald Bain, scholar'; and that though 'Mr Morrison indulges in constant repetition and needless explanations – which are almost necessary in a bard – his matter is good, and he leads to a climax in his narratives with intuitive genius.' 'Domhnull Ban' is also frequently referred to as 'An Sgoilear Bàn', the fair-haired scholar, and was clearly a well-informed, sensitive man with a feeling for drama.[5]

❖

It may have been at the stage when the Macaulays were being hotly pursued by the law that Dòmhnull Cam had to take refuge from his enemies, perhaps in a shelter in South Lochs, in the 'prison' near Barvas, and certainly on the Stac. Matheson then described his predicament as a legally denounced rebel as follows:

'It is also reasonable to suppose that to this period of his life [the first decade or so of the seventeenth century] should be referred the traditions that represent him as an outlaw, dwelling sometimes in the fortalice (dun) on the island in Loch Bharabhat [Uig], and sometimes on the sea-girt rock off the coast at Mangarsta known ever since as Stac Dhòmhnuill Chaim. As long as he was under the ban of the Privy Council it would be prudent to make himself somewhat inaccessible.'[6]

There are indeed two traditions relating to Dòmhnull Cam's days on the Stac. The first tells how the Lewis Chamberlain or factor sent an officer to confiscate some of Dòmhnull's cattle to the value of rent that the 'outlaw' had refused to pay. This officer had to call across to the man on the Stac from the top of the cliff opposite to explain what his mission was. Dòmhnull Cam answered that he could take a suitable number of cattle 'if the herdsman would give them to him.' So the officer went to seize the cattle on their pasture. But Dòmhnull Cam armed himself and went as quickly as he could to where the beasts were grazing and arrived ahead of the officer. When the latter met such a formidable-looking man guarding the cattle he returned to the point opposite the Stac and again found that Dòmhnull Cam was there before him. It appears that the cattle remained where they were undisturbed.

The second tradition about Dòmhnull Cam on the Stac concerns one of his two daughters, thought to have been named Ann or Anna, who, according to the tradition, was much famed for her skill in climbing up the Stac from the narrow connecting ridge when taking food supplies to her father. The tradition known to William Matheson stated 'that she could climb to the top with a pail of milk in each hand'. But Thomas put it rather differently. He said that 'Anna Mhor' or 'Big Anne' used to carry milk and other provisions to Dòmhnull Cam 'over the sharp and dangerous crag which connects the high rock with the mainland.' It was also believed that she carried water on her head in order to leave her hands free to aid her in her climb. Whichever may be the true version, if either, Matheson remarked of it that 'This looks an impossible feat today, but it is said that the configuration of the rock has changed owing to erosion, and also that Dòmhnall Cam had had a series of steps – some of which are still visible – cut out to facilitate the ascent.'[7]

❖

The first and perhaps the best tale told by Donald Morrison covers the career and adventures of Iain Ruadh (John Roy) Macaulay, Dòmhnull Cam's grandfather.[8] The eldest son of Iain Ruadh was called Dùghall (Dugald or Dougal); and Thomas remarked of him that 'the only son of John Roy Macaulay was Dugald, of whom it may be predicated that he had a fortunate life, for nothing is told about him except that he was the father of the famous Lewis champion, Donald Cam Macaulay, and of two other sons who were hardly less remarkable for their courage'. This information about Dugald evidently derives from Morrison's mention of the same man who in addition to Dòmhnull Cam 'had also two other sons, only less remarkable for their bravery'. But it appears from a contemporary and historical record that 'Dughall' had more than three sons. When the group of mainland gentlemen from Fife and their forces came to Lewis about 1600 to assume possession of the island they tried, as Matheson notes, 'to have the family of Dugald MacAulay expelled from Uig, and, on 8th October 1605, we find Rorie MacLeod of Harris entering into an obligation whereby he becomes bound, under penalty of certain sums of money, to see that the sons of Dugald MacAulay and their children, dependants, tenants, and followers, remove themselves and their servants from the lands of Uig'.

This was the first occasion, as noted already, on which the existence of Dòmhnull Cam was historically recorded, and when part of his patronymic, 'mic Dhughaill', son of Dugald, appeared in the roughly phonetic form of 'McCowell', the 'McCoul(l)' of the Dunvegan episode of 1610. The names of the sons, in alphabetical order, were given in the obligation as follows:

'Alister McCowell, Donald McCowell [Dòmhnull Cam], Donald og McCowell, James moir McCowell, James og McCowell, John og McCowell – all brethren vick McCowell'.

Added to this list was another 'Donald McCowell' who was not one of the brothers.

The name of 'James' was unknown among the earlier Macaulays and at that time probably unknown in Lewis, so it has been considered 'a copyist's mistake for some form of Angus'. According to a tradition Dòmhnull Cam had a brother called Angus, though he was not included in the obligation list. Was Dòmhnull Cam the eldest of the brothers? It is not certain that he was, and he was not first in the list, but he was evidently the chief or principal of the brothers in the eyes of the law, 'for

Chapter IV

by boat over the sound, and reached Kirkibost, from which a message was sent to Dòmhnull Cam to tell him what had happened.

'The next day, Donald Cam issued orders to all those living in Uig parish to gather at Kirkibost. This order was obeyed and when the crowd had gathered there, Donald Cam himself appeared, walking from the nearby farm of Balgloum. As Donald Cam was on his way, it was reported to MacPhail that he was coming. MacPhail asked the lookout: "Is he looking up or down as he walks?" The lookout reported that Donald Cam was walking with his eyes looking down on the ground. When he heard this, the prisoner cried mournfully: "Lord, pity my case this day." He added then: "Were MacAulay's eyes now on his way here looking above him to the skies, I would be sure of my life this day. But since his eyes are looking on the earth below, by that I know that there is full revenge determined on."

'Donald Cam had by now arrived at Kirkibost. Without much ceremony it was decreed that MacPhail should be killed by means of every man there who was able to inflict a wound on him with his sword to do so. So MacPhail was now brought out and made to stand on top of a hillock, known since before that day as the Hill of Bad Advice [Creagan na Mi-chomhairle]. The sentence was announced to the doomed man who cried: "The sentence is both unjust and severe. I do not deserve such treatment."[14]

'But Donald Cam MacAulay replied: "A few weeks ago, MacPhail, you, with your own hands, lashed me to the mast of Judge Morrison's yacht [i.e. the Brieve's captured vessel], while others held their swords to my belly. And a few hours later, you, MacPhail, refused to let me answer the call of nature although I pleaded with you to let me do so. But now deserved vengeance will be turned on your head."

'Forthwith, MacAulay ordered the sentence previously decreed to be put into execution. And the following strange thing happened: Men began to thrust their swords at MacPhail and it is said that no fewer than fifty blows were struck to MacPhail's body. But they had no effect. His body appeared invulnerable, and at every blow a kind of vapour ascended from MacPhail's body. The people in the crowd were amazed. Then a pedlar who was looking on said: "Let the grass or ground between MacPhail's feet be cut and that charm now making him proof against every weapon will thus desert him." This was done and MacPhail's body was no longer proof against the sword thrusts and blows. He was killed and his body was slashed to pieces by the swords of all those present at the execution. John Roy MacPhail was no more.'

❖

Probably the best known of the tales about Dòmhnull Cam dealt with his attack on the broch at Carloway, an event that might suggest the continued use of a fortification no longer in its prime. Again Donald Morrison's first notebook is the source of the story, which is a sequel to the quarrel between Dòmhnull Cam and An Gobha Bàn with his red-hot bar of iron. The two, it will be remembered, were reconciled, An Gobha Bàn becoming Dòmhnull Cam's chief henchman in times of difficulty:

'Donald Cam and the Gow Ban went on a trip to the Flannan Isles, during the summer season. The Morrisons of Ness, hearing that Donald was not at home, came across the moor to Uig and stole all the cows belonging to the MacAuleys. None dare resist the Morrisons because Donald Cam and the big blacksmith were not there to lead them. When the men came back from the Flannans, their wives told them what the Morrisons had done.

Chapter IV

Donald Cam and all the men in the boats set off immediately across the channel in an attempt to overtake the stolen herd. As they came in sight of Dun Carloway, they spotted the cattle beside a loch. Guessing that the Morrisons must be inside the strong fortification of the Dun, MacAulay and the Big Smith and crew settled down on a nearby hill for the night.

'Early the following morning, Donald Cam and the big smith crept up to the Dun to surprise the sentry, leaving their crew behind on the hill. The men would need food in order to go on. The first thing Donald and the smith noticed was a large kettle on the fire near the Dun, with a man sleeping beside it. In the kettle, was the best part of a cow's carcass; the Morrisons' breakfast. Donald said to the Gow Ban: "Hold that man while I take the beef out of the kettle." The smith grabbed the sentry and held him fast. Donald took the boiled beef out of the huge kettle and put it in his plaid. Then he threw the cook into the kettle and sent the smith away to feed the men they had left on the hill. This done, he called for the crew to come quickly. Donald Cam then ran up and killed the sentry who was guarding the entrance to the Dun. He told the big smith to stand guard at the door of the Dun. Then Donald Cam began to climb up the walls of the Dun on the outside, using a pair of daggers to help him climb. When he got to the top, he discovered that it was closed by a large flagstone. He then called down to his men to pull heather from the moor and to pass it up to him. He made bundles of this heather and filled the top room of the Dun with it. This done, he set the heather on fire and replaced the flagstone. The smoke and heat from the blazing heather smothered the men inside the Dun: they could not escape through the door because it was guarded.

'Now Donald Cam and his men demolished this old Dun at Carloway, built in the Fourth Century by a giant called Darge

MacNuaran. There are two similar Duns in Uig, and they were built by Darge's brothers, Cuoch and Tid MacNuaran, who lived in them. One Dun is at Uig, the other at Kirkibost.'

❖

These tales falling into what has here been called 'the first category' tell of Dòmhnull Cam's adventures and in so doing certainly reflect a good deal upon his character. But those of the second kind do so rather more vividly and tend to emphasise the vicious streak in Dòmhnull Cam. One such episode is the story of the blind old woman, as told by Donald Morrison:

'Donald Cam and the Big Blacksmith [i.e. An Gobha Ban] at Kneep were walking together when they passed by a small bothy in which an old blind woman lived.

'Some of the tenants' wives were sitting close by. One of the women said: "These two men are extraordinary men. There can be few like them in the country. We need not be afraid should an enemy attempt to invade or plunder us." On hearing this, the poor blind woman within the little hut asked who these men were, that they praised so much. She was told they were Donald Cam and the Big Smith. The blind woman then exclaimed indignantly "Hush! Were you to have seen those men that fought the Battle of Machair House at Reef! I say – had you seen those heroes who repulsed and killed a Danish pirate and his crew, you would not say that either Donald Cam or the smith are men of great valour or prowess!" On hearing the talk, the two men enquired: "What does the old blind woman say?" The women told them. They then fell to and shut up the door of the bothy with stones and threatened instant death to any person who would give any food or anything else to the old blind woman but let her starve. It is said that she soon did so.

plus a little extra. To this the woman agreed and left the meal with the tenants of Dell.

'When she returned to Uig, her foster son asked her what success she had had in Ness. She replied that the tenants of Dell had imposed on her to give them what meal she had got in Ness – and had given her nothing in return. On hearing this, Donald Cam set out for Ness and arrived at Dell. He found the poor tenants gathering shellfish down in the ebb shore, for food, as these were scanty years. Donald now waited for them to come to the land and let his unsuspecting victims approach. It is said that he put no question to them: simply ordered them to dig their own graves on the spot.

'Then Donald Cam killed all six of them and buried them there. We must partly blame his foster mother for this merciless act of Donald Cam's.'

The second story was set at Brenish in Uig where Angus Macaulay, a son of Dòmhnull Cam, was tenant of the farm. At Christmas one year Angus invited the family to come and stay with him at Brenish, and this they did.

'One day, a fortune teller came to the house, while the MacAulays were enjoying themselves in the main room. The palmister was left in the kitchen. The fortune teller was not pleased with the welcome he got in Angus MacAulay's house. He told the servants: "The landlord of this house will not enjoy any more Christmases in this life." This statement came to the good wife's ears through the servants. Her face at once showed the trouble in her mind and all the guests observed that she was worried. Her husband asked her what was wrong. She was very unwilling to tell, but they all insisted that she let them know what was troubling her. She then told them what the palmist had said in the kitchen regarding her husband's short life.

'Donald Cam then told the mistress to go to the fortune teller and ask him how many years he, the fortune teller, expected to live thereafter. The mistress went down to the kitchen and asked this question of the fortune teller. He looked into the palm of his hand and said: "A good many years yet. I expect to live long." Donald Cam then said: "If that be true, this is not true." He held up his hand gun. Then he rose to go to the kitchen. Some of the servants told the fortune teller: "Run! Escape!" The palmist ran out of the house with Donald Cam in pursuit. He caught him up near the house and shot him, on a plain since known as Leub an Darnidar or the Palmister's Rig.'[16]

❖

The tales recorded by Donald Morrison also introduced another character to the drama of island life in the days of Dòmhnull Cam. At a time when the Macaulays and Morrisons had stopped feuding for a while there arrived at Barra a heavily armed ship which, it was believed, had come 'to subjugate the Long Island clans and to punish the guilty'. In the face of such a threat the Lewis factions decided to unite and depart for Barra in three large boats, one of which pertained to the Brieve. They reached their destination and the next day boarded the mysterious ship with consequences described by the cooper Morrison:

'They killed all they found on board her, with the exception of one man, his wife and child. These three the Lewismen spared, because they discovered that they could speak Gaelic. On board they found a great deal of wealth, plus arms of all descriptions, including cannon and shot. The Lewis clans took away as much as they could load on board their boats, leaving the rest to the neighbouring clans. So they returned with their booty, bringing to Uig with them, John Du Craig and his parents, for he was the child that had been spared on board this ship. This is the way in which John Du Craig came to Lewis.'

It seems that the ship was an English one and that following the assault on it soldiers were sent to Lewis where they were all killed by Dòmhnull Cam and others – possibly Macleods. Having his share of the booty from the ship but being a wanted man Dòmhnull Cam took cannon and 'military stores' and 'went to a rock to the west of Uig, where he built a battery of guns'. It was at this time that Neil Macleod resorted for much the same purpose to the cliff-bound island of Berisay on the way out of Loch Roag beyond Bernera.

Soon another strange ship appeared, this time in Loch Roag, where it anchored at 'Enishgary' near Kirkibost. News of this was circulated widely, particularly because it was thought 'that one of the highest statesmen in the land, suspected of disloyalty at Court, had made escape with this ship'. So the leaders of the three main Lewis clans, the Brieve (Morrisons), Dòmhnull Cam (Macaulays) and Neil Macleod, assembled some men and on reaching Kirkibost boarded this ship. Seeing nothing of the supposed statesman they then left but posted some look-outs on the shore to keep watch on the ship:

'On the third day, the clans managed to catch some salmon in the Grimersta river. These fish, they placed alive in a large hogshead filled with water. Large spike nails had been driven through the bottom of the cask. One of the leaders went out to the ship with this cask of live fish. The ship's crew were so excited by the sight of the live salmon in the cask that the noise on deck attracted the attention of the statesman below. He came up on deck and looked into the cask. The clansmen suddenly grabbed him by the legs and dumped him into the cask, drowning him and killing him with the nails in the bottom of the cask. Then the Lewismen killed all on board and plundered the ship. It is said that there was a vast amount of gold on board; so much of it that they used Donald Cam's helmet as a measure, when they came to share it out.'

As a result of this incident a 'battleship' was sent to Lewis and Stornoway Castle was captured. Dòmhnull Cam and two of his brothers succeeded in regaining the castle, though one of the brothers was 'killed by a shot from the defenders while [he was] standing on South Beach'. Dòmhnull Cam was so outraged at this that he took a blacksmith's hammer and broke down the gates of the castle so that the Lewismen could get inside. 'The few English who escaped with their lives fled back south.' And Dòmhnull Cam and Neil Macleod retreated to the strongholds which they had prepared and armed beforehand.

❖

John Du Craig, the young lad taken with his parents from the ship at Barra, had been chosen by Dòmhnull Cam as his personal servant and is said to have been the ancestor of the Mackinnons of Lewis. The one story about Dòmhnull Cam which does not involve real violence and which even suggests that the Macaulay had a sense of humour tells how the two men were involved in a boat adventure in Uig:

'At one time, Donald Cam and John Du Craig had to go into hiding on an island in Uig, on a loch called Loch Barravat, a few miles west of the manse at Uig and where there is still to be seen the ruins of a house or dun. Leading to this island across the water on the north side, are stones laid in a straight line; that is, those of the stones as are always above water. But the stepping stones that lie under water are deliberately laid crookedly to one side of the path, so as to make strangers fall into the water, if they try to cross to the island by night, for instance.

Chapter IV

'Donald Cam and John Du Craig lived on this island for a time, subsisting chiefly on fish and venison. They also had a boat with which they fished at Gallon Head now and then. When not in use, this boat was dragged inshore for some distance and hidden, so that an enemy could not use it to cross to the island. One day, while they were fishing with long lines, John was rowing the boat while his master was taking in the lines. The wind was fairly strong at the time. Donald Cam said to John Du: "Pull the boat ahead better!" John was doing all he could and replied: "Better, I can't. What I can't do, do it yourself." At this, Donald Cam let go of the lines and drew his dagger. John Du knew what was coming and immediately threw both oars over the side of the boat and jumped into the water after them. John Du immediately swam for the beach known as Moll na h-Arde, or Beach of Aird. From there, he made his way home to the Island on the loch, put on a good fire and swept the floor of the house. His master was tossed about in the boat until he finally managed to recover the oars. He took up the lines and rowed ashore, much dejected, for he thought he had lost John Du, imagining him to have been drowned. But as he came in sight of the house on the island, he was overjoyed to see smoke ascending from the chimney of the house. Donald Cam went in, found John sitting by a roaring fire and noticed that the house had been swept and cleaned. He sat down and warmed himself and then said: "You foolish lad, what made you deprive me of the oars?" John replied: "Had I left you the oars in the boat, I might as well have stopped there myself." He added that he had considered this the only effective way open to him, to escape the effects of Donald Cam's anger. It was the only method by which he could deprive MacAulay of the chance to execute his violent passions. Donald Cam smiled but only said: "Make the supper, John."'

It was said that John Du was so skilled with the short sword that he could hold off Dòmhnull Cam, but that he was not strong enough to wield the broadsword to such effect.[17]

❖

What, in summary, can be said of Dòmhnull Cam? There is no doubt that he existed in authentic record, evidently during a period extending to either side of 1600, and that he was exceptional enough in reputation and in exploits and adventures to attract a larger body of traditions relating his deeds than any other person in Lewis history. He is an outstanding figure among the Macaulays of Uig, but not necessarily an attractive one, and according to Donald Morrison's account of the 'Red Weaver', he inspired terror far and wide. 'There are so many traits in the conduct of this hero,' remarked Morrison at the end of the fortune teller story, 'that are revolting to ordinary humanity that we in our own days ought to be thankful to that divine power who alone has dispelled such barbarous darkness and oppression from our land.' Yet the tales were told, the traits described, and in much more recent times Matheson wrote that 'Some of the stories told about him are sufficiently grim, depicting as they do a man whose sudden bursts of fury made life uncertain for those, even of his own following, who gave the least cause of offence.'

Though he committed various violent acts and apparently 'lived the life of an outlaw' at one stage, Dòmhnull Cam seems to have been pardoned for his offensive behaviour and in his later years to have turned his attention to the more peaceful activity of farming his lands in Uig. As Donald Morrison tells, he eventually 'enjoyed undisturbed repose in Uig from enemies without' and 'bye and bye he died – a middle-aged man'.

but on the whole he accepted tradition as a good preserver of historical episodes and as worthy of trust, though with an appropriate amount of caution. And perhaps that is the best way to look upon the association of Dòmhnull Cam with the three coastal locations, and with the great whale washed up at Dalbeg – which is another story best told elsewhere.

References and Notes

(Endnotes)

1. NRS E655/1/2; E655/2/2; E655/3; GD427/1
2. F W L Thomas: 'On the Duns of the Outer Hebrides' in <u>Archaeologia Scotica</u> Vol.V p.395
3. For the access and archaeological information given here – see C S Barrowman, I McHardy, & M Macleod: <u>Severe Terrain Archaeological Campaign (STAC) Rope Access and Topographical Survey</u> – Unpublished interim report 2004 Section 7
4. W Matheson: 'History of the Macaulays' (Second Series Pt.3) in <u>SG</u> 19 February 1957. See also First series Pt.2 in <u>SG</u> 2 October 1956. F W L Thomas: 'Traditions of the Macaulays of Lewis' in <u>P.S.A.S.</u> 14 June 1880 pp.384, 414. Thomas's quotation from the 'Gregory Collections, MS.' adds that the intention of the Privy Council at the meeting on 31 May 1611 had been to 'give such other directions anent them as shall seem most meet and expedient for the quietness of the country'. Thomas thought that it was at this time that Dòmhnull Cam 'fortified himself' on the Stac
5. Thomas: 'Traditions of the Macaulays of Lewis' pp.385-386
6. Matheson: 'History of the Macaulays' (First Series Pt.4) in <u>SG</u> 16 October 1956
7. Thomas: 'Traditions of the Macaulays of Lewis' p.413; and 'On the Duns of the Outer Hebrides' pp.395-396.
8. Matheson: 'History of the MacAulays' (First Series Pt.4) in <u>SG</u> 16 October 1956
9. Matheson: 'History of the MacAulays' (First Series Pt.4) in <u>SG</u> 16 October 1956
10. This tale, with others quoted here, is published in N Macdonald: <u>The Morrison Manuscript – Traditions of the Western Isles by Donald Morrison, Cooper, Stornoway</u> Stornoway 1975 pp.19-21. Dòmhnull Cam's horse may have been an old one driven over the cliff, as this

means of disposing of redundant horses was widely practised in Lewis at suitable places indicated and still known by such names as 'Geodha nan Each'

11 Matheson [(Macaulays – Second Series Pt.1) in <u>SG</u> 29 January 1957] has a note about the song: 'No song of this name is now known, but it may be that the reference is to a pibroch. There are in fact two pibrochs that come to mind in this connection, one known as "Ceann na Drochaide Moire", and the other as "Ceann na Drochaide Bige", though it has been claimed for both of them that they celebrate events in the history of the MacDonalds. We also find an item called "Ceann Drochaid Alainn" in a list of pipe tunes associated with the Clan MacKenzie'

12 Thomas, drawing upon Morrison's account, added a note at this point, 'Traditions of the Macaulays of Lewis' (p.401): 'The iron chain was kept for many years at Dunvegan as a convincing proof of the strength and endurance of Donald Cam; but once, when Macleod was from home, a blacksmith converted it to some domestic use. The late Rev. Hugh Munro, of Uig, saw the chain at Dunvegan when it weighed eleven (Dutch) stones'

13 Iain Ruadh MacPhail was also known as Iain Mòr MacKay, and it was by this name that he appeared in Thomas's version of the story (pp.401-403)

14 For Creagan na Mì-chomhairle see D Macaulay: 'Studying the place names of Bernera' in <u>TGSI</u> XLVII (1971-72) pp.313-337. Thomas, 'Traditions of the Macaulays of Lewis' (p.404) calls the hill 'Cnoc na mi-Chomhairle' but notes, not quite accurately, that 'Cnocan na mi-Chomhairle' is marked on the OS six inch map of 1853 (corr. Cnocan na mi-Chomhairl)

15 Matheson was of the view that the battle with the Danish pirate who landed at Reef was not sufficient reason for the action taken by Dòmhnull Cam and the smith. He said that 'this explanation does not carry conviction' and went on: 'If, as one supposes, the inhabitants included MacAulays, Domhnull Cam's rage is scarcely comprehensible. After all, the men of former generations have always been represented as mightier than their descendants. One thought that may occur .. is that early in Domhnull Cam's life very old people could remember the events of 1506'

16 Thomas, 'Traditions of the Macaulays of Lewis' (p.415), as usual drew upon Morrison for this story but made one or two additions. After he had been told what the 'palmister' had said Dòmhnull Cam 'took hold of the Chaum, a name which he gave to his gun', and shot the fortune teller 'at a spot since then called Leob a Phalmaistear, or the Palmister's Rig'

17 Thomas altered 'John Du Craig' to 'John Du Chroig' (Black John of the big fist) and the name of the loch from 'Loch Barravat' to 'Loch Burravat' which he said meant 'Castle-lake'. 'This name', he noted, 'always indicates the existence of a Pictish tower'. Matheson identified the site of the island house as in 'Loch Bharabhat'

Chapter V
Plane lands on Rona

The small island of Rona lies about 40 miles north of the lighthouse at the Butt of Lewis. These days it is commonly called North Rona, probably to distinguish it from two other islands known by the same name, one off Kallin in Grimsay between North Uist and Benbecula, the other off the north tip of Raasay, east of Skye.

Before the arrival of early nineteenth century travellers with their inclination to invent their own names for places, Rona, out amid the great swelling seas towards the Faroe Islands and Iceland, was properly called Rona of the Ocean, or rather 'Ronaidh an t-haf', a name derived from the Norse and taken partly into Gaelic but curiously ignored today. Until around 1700 the island had a native population which restricted its numbers to about thirty owing to the very limited capacity of the island to support them. The people lived in a settlement built of stone and turf, and sunk into the south-facing slope where the ground was fertile and able to produce crops of grain and hay. A few cattle and sheep grazed there, and breeding sea-birds in the summer were an important additional source of food along with the fish that could be caught from the rocky shores or possibly from a small boat.

The grass was bent towards the east or north-east and laid flat by westerly gales through the winter, but as the spring arrived there was a tendency for the wind to turn easterly and shrivel new growth with a dry, cold and salt-laden blast. Today, but with less regularity, the same weather pattern still prevails. In these conditions migrant birds often seek shelter among the remains of the tumbled walls of the dwellings and in the recesses of ancient cells and chapels. Until the beginning of May Rona is reluctant to emerge from its hibernation, but winter and summer alike it has never been without remarkable events that have featured in and indeed formed its history. In the brown depths of December and the green heights of June the Rona story spreads itself enticingly over those who visit it and even over those who have only heard of it, just as the blended scents of sea spray, storm petrels and fork-tailed petrels, and pink thrift stir the imagination of those who would like to go there again.

❖

One of the most remarkable of the 'incidents' in the story of Rona was that which took place in the spring of 1941.[1] Though the details are not widely known, it has given rise to a number of rumours.

It began on 23 April, when a strong east wind was raising the sea and forcing the lesser birds to take refuge on land if they could reach any. Being war-time the islands of Rona and its neighbour, Sulasgeir, were 'out of bounds', isolated in their loneliness. But aircraft were never too far away, some of them operating from the airfield near Wick in Caithness, which was much nearer to Orkney and Shetland than to the north-west extremities of the Hebrides. At the time, '612 County of Aberdeen Squadron' was based at Wick. It had very recently been equipped with Whitley planes 'fitted with the then most modern and secret device known as ASV (Anti Surface Vessel)', a form of radar. The use of such equipment 'entailed carrying large cumbersome aerials on the underside of each wing which detracted greatly from the aircraft's performance and made it difficult to fly on one engine'. Secrecy required that a Whitley carrying the ASV should be thought to be a bomber.

Chapter V

Early in the morning of 23 April 1941 a Whitley took off from Wick. It was piloted by the Squadron's commanding officer, Wing Commander John B M Wallis, known as 'Winkie', who later became Air Commodore Wallis and in 1971 was resident in Cape Province, South Africa, where he had been living for twelve years. On 28 July 1971 he wrote a letter describing what happened on that day thirty years earlier.

'I decided to test the ASV as a homing device on the Wick MF/DF beacon which we reckoned would work from about 60 to 80 miles distance. I therefore chose N. RONA as the turning point as this island is exactly 100 miles from Wick. There was a roaring EAST wind coming down the Pentlands, but a clear cloudless sky and a very violent sea.

'All went well until we came to the Island when the 2nd Pilot F/O Hatchwell suddenly and excitedly pointed to the under part of the Port engine forward by the propeller where oil was gushing out. My heart sank as I knew exactly what had happened – the oil pipe from the engine to the Variable pitch unit in the propeller had fractured and there was less than 10 mins flying left on that engine. This had happened to me in a Whitley in Feb. when flying between CASTLETOWN and HATSTON but I was able to get it back to WICK before the engine went on fire. I managed to put it out with the GRAVINER switch and land on one engine.

'I knew therefore what the problem was and that there were 5 possible ways of dealing with it:-

1. Try to fly back to Wick, most of it would be on one engine against a roaring East Wind. Quite bluntly this was not on.
2. Try for Stornoway about 80 miles SW and slightly down wind. Better than (1) above but very chancy.

3. Land in the sea and take to our rubber Dinghies and hope we would be picked up. But the sea was so rough that this was right out.
4. Fly to the mainland (Cape Wrath). But where to land on what would be for a certainty one engine was a problem.
5. Land on N. RONA itself – barely ½ mile long very rugged and undulating.

'I chose N. Rona and my choice had to be pretty quick, a matter of a few seconds, as we were only 1500 feet up and with the Port Engine throttled back we were starting to lose height.

'Orders were quickly given for the crew to take up ditching stations and for the war load to be jettisoned. I made a left hand circuit into the East wind. As both engines were still working I came in under power with both but just as I came over the western edge of the Island, Hatchwell shouted to me that my flaps were not down, so down they went full.'

In addition to the pilot there were five other crew members in the aircraft, but no navigator. It had been the intention that a navigator, Sergeant Arthur Stone, should come along but he changed his mind because, in spite of the strong wind, the weather was so clear and bright and he did not think the journey worthwhile. Those who did accompany Wing Commander Wallis were Flying Officer Hatchwell, Pilot Officer Henson, and George Archer, William Foots and A Mathers, all Sergeants. They must have been filled with nervous anticipation when they learned what the pilot intended to do.

Wallis's letter continued:
'At the Eastern end of the Island there is a slight Knoll of say 100 feet with sheer drops of many hundreds of feet into the sea

on the E. N and S. On the Western side of the Knoll there was a small area of pastureland about 200 yards long east to west. [To] the West of this pastureland was some very rough ground with what appeared to be boulders strewn about and to the north of this was a dilapidated Crofters Cottage.

'My aim was the pastureland which appeared smooth. With both engines going steadily I descended slowly and finally cut them right back in front of the Cottage. Just before landing I had a ghastly few seconds when a gust of wind came round the north side of the Knoll and lifted my port wing and blew me towards the South side. I had enough forward speed to right the aircraft and put it down lightly just over the border from the rough ground.

'I just had to make it – failure would have been fatal to us all.

'The very high wind on that day was our saving grace. Our ground speed could not have been more than 40 Knots.

'As soon as we came to a stop after sliding on our belly with the wheels up for a short distance the ignition and petrol were switched off and every one got out quickly fearing that fire might break out.'

Because Wallis was unfamiliar with the terrain of Rona and with the remains of buildings, his description of the 'Knoll' and of the 'dilapidated Crofters Cottage' is too vague to permit accurate identification of what he was talking about. The 'Knoll' could have been either the 'Toa', the highest ground of the island at 348 feet, or possibly the sharply pointed and rocky 'knoll' (known formerly as Sìthean a Croer) above the slope down to Fianuis. As there was never a 'crofter's cottage' of the usual form as known on Lewis, the structure so called could have been the ruined chapel and cell or merely the walls of the old settlement glimpsed as the landing aircraft sped by. As for the apparently 'smooth' pastureland, this would suggest that the sliding plane may have by good fortune missed the extremely bumpy area of cultivation ridges (feannagan) but considerable damage was caused to the forward end underside of the fuselage by a 'bank' with rocks and 'stone circles' at intervals along it.

'After a lapse of about 5 minutes we returned to the aircraft and found that the W/T (Wireless Transmitter) was working so we got in Touch with WICK and told them our story. Wick ordered an Air Sea Rescue launch from KIRKWALL to come to our rescue. This launch came like the hobs of hell downwind and made the Island in just 4 hours which was good going. Meanwhile Aircraft were despatched to patrol the Island and see that no attempt was made by enemy submarines to land a party on the Island and take off our most secret ASV.

'None of the crew were hurt and we took up stations around the Island to watch for the rescue launch or any enemy submarines that might be too curious.

'At that time of my life I sported a very fierce handlebar moustache (the original RAF prototype) and I was told by one of the crew that he saw one of the many seals there surface Salute and say "Good-morning, Sir" !!!

'The launch duly arrived and found a small protected inlet on the westward and leeward side of the Island. I cannot remember exactly if they came alongside a natural jetty or sent a dinghy to fetch us.

'The weather was still bad – very high east wind and violent sea, so the Captain of the launch suggested we should stay the night and go back next morning by which time the storm might have abated. As I had had enough adventure for one day I readily agreed. Our journey back next morning was uneventful. We were landed at THURSO harbour where the Wick Station Commander Group Captain Drew gave us a warm welcome.'

Chapter V

❖

The remaining difficulty was how to deal with the crashed aircraft, its secret ASV equipment, and parts of the plane which could be of value and perhaps brought back into use. As he wrote in his letter, Wallis did not remember much of what happened.

'I do not know much about the Salvage operations except that since at that time of the war Merlin Engines were desperately needed and as both Engines did not appear to have been too badly damaged by the landing they were worth salvaging. Thinking back there was also not much damage to the aircraft and in any case there was a considerable amount of equipment that could be used again.

'In the event a Trawler was commissioned to do the Salvage job.'

Those responsible for the recovery of the Whitley were men of the No.63 Maintenance Unit at RAF Carluke, beside Glasgow. Two groups of a mobile recovery party, consisting in all of one officer, six NCOs, and about twenty airmen, were ordered to go to Rona under the command of Pilot Officer A C Davis, who was later awarded the MBE for his skill and leadership during the whole operation. They travelled north to Scrabster in the first week of May 1941 and went on board the trawler, named HMS *Preston North End*, which was armed and already provided with recovery equipment and other necessary supplies.

At 9.30am on 7 May the adapted trawler was lying close to the south coast of Rona and those on board could clearly see the plane resting on the grass not far up the gentle slope from the deep inlet in the cliffs called Poll Thothatom. The senior N.C.O. of the salvage party, Desmond C F Waller, and Pilot Officer Davis then circumnavigated the island, looking 'for a spot that would lend itself to easy landing of our heavy equipment', which included tents, food, water, arms, and, in case wireless transmission was not normally allowed, carrier pigeons. Having decided upon the inlet of Poll Thothatom as a suitable landing place, Pilot Officer Davis and Lieutenant Vasey were able to get ashore there and they then climbed up to make a preliminary study of the job facing them. All that day the recovery equipment was unloaded, taken ashore and placed near the Whitley, while the three camouflaged tents and other items needed for living on the island were conveyed to the ruined buildings of the old settlement where some shelter was available. A cookhouse was set up in the westmost ruin which had been a grain-drying kiln in days when Rona was inhabited, and the tents were erected nearby. Dark, partly-roofed cells, substantial sections of stone walls, and passages still formed reasonably intact evidence of how the people had constructed their dwellings and protected themselves from rain and gales.

A machine gun post was established and kept permanently manned in case of unexpected intrusion.

Davis sent reports on the condition of the Whitley and, especially, on the engines and fractured pipelines. The principal task was to remove the ASV, but in the course of preliminary work it was decided to try to recover the entire aircraft as well. So the ASV and the pipelines were taken out first and put on board the trawler which then left on return to the mainland. That was in the late evening of 8 May, and, as the first task, was safely accomplished.

It then took a week to dismantle the plane, work which included removal of the important engines, separating the wings, and dividing the fuselage into three parts. Waller remembered that 'Each section then was carefully marked and protected against possible damage', likely to occur 'whilst being lowered from the cliffs to the lighter below at sea level or to subsequent transportation risks'. As it turned out wireless contact was maintained all the time so that any specialist advice could be promptly supplied to Davis, and of course security guard with the aid of machine gun, rifles and pistols was kept in accordance with the operation order: 'Continuous lookout is to be maintained. The machine gun post is to be continually manned with guns loaded.' And 'if airing of bedding is resorted to, care is to be taken to select suitable spaces to ensure against the enemy observing that the Island is occupied'. It might have been thought that the plane itself and the action around it would have been sufficient to draw the enemy's attention.

❖

While the salvage crew were at work on the island the converted trawler *Preston North End* and an armed drifter, HMS *Mist*, made occasional visits when weather allowed with food supplies and other useful gear, and since it was early summer those men ashore who felt like it could raid gulls' nests and fry the eggs as they did when food ran short. But near the beginning of the period during which the Whitley was prepared for removal there occurred another incident which has probably become the best known episode of the whole operation. In his letter, many years later, Air Commodore Wallis included a short and very inaccurate description:

'I was told that during the Salvage operation the Salvage crew found the Skeleton of a man right up at the top of the hill above the cottage where there was some sort of Cairn with a pole on it. Obviously some sailor who was washed on the Island in an exhausted state and managed to get to the top where he died from exposure. As there was no means of identifying him they buried him up there under the name of GEORGE RONA.'

Long after the actual Whitley event on Rona a second version of this tale began to circulate, even more astray from the truth than that told by Wallis. It was rumoured that the body of a German naval officer had been found by the salvage party in one of the ruined huts of the settlement. The officer was said to have been in full uniform, complete with hat, and beside him a H/F radio set. His back was against a wall, and to all appearances he had arrived on the island as if by intended landing. In his book *Shillay and the Seals*, published in 1980, Robert Atkinson wrote of how a yachtsman, Dr Robert Morrison, when somewhere on the mainland, once gave a lift to a total stranger who happened to have been one of the salvage group. From him Morrison heard about the German, and in due course the story appeared in the *Stornoway Gazette*. But of course it was not a true account of what had really happened back in 1941.

It seems that only a few hours after occupying the western edge of the settlement ruins LAC Michael Johnson 'noticed a putrid smell coming from one of the ruined bothies near the camp site' and along with two others went to investigate.

'There they found the semi-mummified blackened remains of a sailor lying flat on his back with his feet at the bothy entrance. They reckoned that he had probably been dead for between two and five months ... He was wearing navy blue cloth trousers, similar to service material, with plain straight legs and bottoms (not bell bottoms), and a jacket or coat of the same material. No buttons or badges were obvious; the jacket was buttoned up to the neck and there was no sign of a shirt or sweater. He was wearing black boots. Lieutenant Vasey made a thorough search of the body – not a pleasant task – but, with neither dog tags nor identification documents, it was impossible to put a name to the poor individual.'

in the pasture to show where the plane had landed, and, though he did not then know of the burial of the dead sailor, no sign of the remains of 'George Rona'. It had been, as Air Commodore Wallis put it, 'a mighty fine effort'. In the conclusion of his letter Wallis recollected his own experience in words to match: 'So ends my story about an episode that was one of the most exciting events of my life.' And Waller also commented on the whole event: 'Although my expedition to Rona was one of many in strange places, I shall never forget standing on the headland in the wind watching the seals, and the considerable bird life, and wondering why people ever thought it fit for human habitation.'

The salvage team outside the cookhouse, Rona

Note

(Endnotes)
1   I am grateful to Roger Atkinson, whose uncle was an active participant in the incident, for the loan of papers and photographs covering this Rona episode. (It is to be noted that Roger is not a relative of the Robert Atkinson quoted in the above account)

Salvage team on watch practice, armed and ready to defend the island

Chapter VI
Airidh na h-Aon Oidhche

A leading merchant family, the Jollys, operating from Leith and one or two other ports nearby such as Prestonpans in the 1660s, possessed a ship trading sometimes as far as London on their own behalf as well as for others in the same business. This ship was called the Black Dog, perhaps not an unusual name for vessels in the world of marine merchant activities at that time or later, and occurring even in tales of seafaring adventure, true or imaginative.[1] In an early chapter of Robert Louis Stevenson's *Treasure Island* the acquaintance is made of Captain Billy Bones who apparently had a black dog tattooed on his back. And at a similar stage of the story one of the first strikingly threatening characters who abruptly arrived at the 'Admiral Benbow' inn and departed as quickly was a pirate, 'a pale, tallowy creature, wanting two fingers of the left hand'. His name was Black Dog.

Returning to the not-so-different sphere of fact in place of fiction the seas north of the Butt of Lewis were, as they had long been, great fishing grounds visited by boats from the distant east coast of England and from other countries as well as by local craft out from Stornoway and the unfinished harbour at Port of Ness. On or about 12 August 1884 a boat builder and fisherman from Port, Murdo Macleod, and his crew of three, were looking to catch cod near the Butt when they saw two strange boats, one at least of which was very old with shabby, worn sails and looked as though it had frequently been repaired. Two of Murdo's crew spoke to the people on board, eight of them, who were mostly dark of complexion, 'very rough looking, and very uncivil'. Along with them was something else that added to the inhospitable

Airidh na h-Aon Oidhche

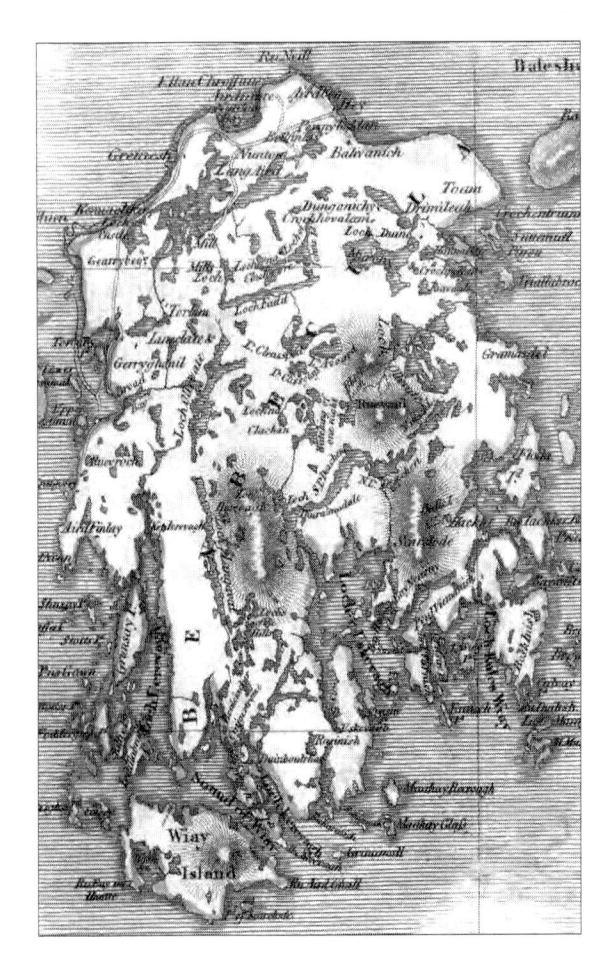

*Maps of Benbecula 1822, with 'Watching of the One Night'
to left of 'Ruevaul'*

areas of England, and apparently in western Scotland. More than sixty years ago in Wales 'There was a general understanding that if a house was raised during the night so that the builders were able to cause smoke to issue from the chimney by sunrise, they therefore established a right of possession which none can gainsay'. The house was called in Welsh 'Ty un nos', the one-night house, otherwise known as 'Hafod-un-nos' and 'Caban-un-nos'; and one of the French equivalents was a 'Jasserie', a hut built in the summer pastures for the herdsman of cattle taken to the higher ground. Moreover, in a letter from Stornoway, sent in or about 1941, a Miss Annie Macleod wrote that 'It seems to be quite a common idea in the islands and west coast of Scotland, that, if a house is built in one night on waste ground and smoke rises from it by dawn, the builder establishes his right to it freehold, and as long as that fire is kept alight no one can evict him'. Certainly, the idea seems to have existed in the vicinity of Barra:

'There is a story that one of the [Vatersay] raiders completed building a dwelling and had a fire lit in it in one day, which entitled him, under an old law, to remain in occupation of the house. There is such a law, but no mention of this has been found in any of the reports at the time or in the following years, so it is uncertain.'

The widespread nature of the belief in the house of one night may suggest that it was a very old one, and the similarity with certain aspects of the building, locations and purpose of shieling huts may indicate that at one time in the remote past the two customs had a common origin. However, as the stories associated with a 'shieling of one night' seem to show, there is apparently no more recent connection between the 'Ty un nos' and the 'Airidh na h-Aon Oidhche', which were certainly not the same thing, and the former offers nothing by way of an explanation for the emergence of those stories. Yet it is possible that at some point long ago there was a link and it is worth visualising the custom of the one-night house somewhere in the background to those shielings that have such a similar name.[7]

❖

At least four different versions of the tale told much later by Peter MacCormick were heard and recorded on paper in Gaelic and English by Alexander Carmichael in Benbecula in the second half of 1871. They share similar features and seem to have been widely known in the island. Perhaps they had descended over the centuries from one generation to another of people like Peter MacCormick and had been subject only to the incidental changes introduced by the individual storytellers who inherited them. Carmichael seems to have handed over copies of his four versions to Captain F W L Thomas, who wrote them out again and gave them the English form in which they survive. Some of the notes attached were by Carmichael, others added by Thomas. For the sake of a fuller picture rather than worrying about the repetition, all versions are given below.[8]

According to Carmichael the following first version came 'from a Benbecula man, a fellow traveller along the road in Benbecula, one day in July, 1871':

The One Night's Shieling
Arri na h-aon Oiche

A man of the name of Macphie lived in Benbecula, and he was a man of some substance and position. He had a black dog, and the dog grew up a large powerful animal. The dog never barked. Every person was expressing surprise at the dog's silence, and at

Macphie for keeping him. But Macphie would only remark that the black dog's day had not yet come – 'Gun robh la coin duigh gun tighinn fhathast' (See note below).

Time wore on, and Macphie, who was known as Macphie of the Black Dog – Macaphie a choin dugh – built a summer shieling – airri shamhrai – When the shieling was finished Macphie and his twelve foster-brothers repaired to it for recreation and sport. The black dog faithfully followed Macphie, and he was along with him on this occasion.

When they lay down at night on their couches of heath, they wished that they had their sweethearts along with them.

'Don e! don e! dh-iarr sibh a chomhaltair.' 'Bad, bad, it is you have asked, my foster-brothers,' said Macphie, and he flew out of the shealing, to the astonishment of his men, and followed by his dog. He had scarcely left, when in rushed twelve witches with bone beaks and green dresses. They flew at the throats of the twelve fosterbrothers and with their bone beaks immediately sucked them dry.

Another of the witches flew after Macphie, who was on his way home. She soon came up with him, and when he discovered that the 'Taislig' was getting near him he set the dog at it. 'Stiuge 'n cu innte,' – and although the dog never showed fight before, he rushed at the creature (creatair) with unbounded ferocity. Macphie continued his fleet career homewards, where he soon arrived. In the course of time the dog arrived homeward also, totally devoid of hair and raving mad. Four boynes of milk were set before him, three of which he lapped, and then burst.

A number of people went out to the shealing early in the morning, when they found Macphie's twelve fosterbrothers stiff and dead, with holes in their throats and their blood sucked dry by the witches of the bone beaks and green dresses. The shealing was never more used, and it has ever been known since, and ever will be known to the son yet unborn as the One Night's Shealing – Arri na h-aon Oidhe.

Note. It is said this was the origin of the proverb – 'Tha la choin duigh gun tighinn fhathast' – 'The black dog's day is not yet come' – when applied to a thing or person whose usefulness is not particularly marked. 'Tha la fhinn aig a chude cu' – 'Every dog has his day' – needs no explanation.

❖

Two of the remaining three versions collected by Alexander Carmichael are dated 13 December 1871 and the third the day after, but it is not certain that they were all told to him within these two days. They contain interesting variations from and additions to that he heard from the man on the road the previous July, in particular the Gaelic verse in the exchange between the men in the shieling and the visiting woman included in the version given by 'James Macinnon, crofter, Bailevanaich, Benbecula, S.Uist':

Airi na h-aon Oiche
or
The Sheiling of One Night

Macphie of the black dog had the whole of Uacar (a farm in Benbecula – A.C.) to himself, and he sent his men to build a shieling (airi). The men built the shealing, and sat down to warm themselves at the fire before going to bed. While the men were warming themselves before the fire a curious-looking little woman walked in and sat down beside them. There was something very curious about the little woman, and although all the men knew all the women in the district none recognized this strange looking little carlin.

The men prepared to lie down on their pallets of rushes, and when the strange carlin saw this she said –

> 'Suidhe, suidhe, suidhegan,
> Laidhe, laidhe, laidhegan,
> Cait an caidil cailleachag bheag bhoc?'

> i.e. 'Sit, sit, sitting,
> Lie, lie, lying;
> Where will poor little carlin sleep tonight?'

'You will lie beside the fire,' said the men.

> 'Beiridh biast an tein orm.
> Laidhe, laidhe, laidhegan
> Suidhe, suidhe, suidhegan
> Cat an caidil cailleachag bheag bhoc?'

> 'The beast of the fire will catch me.
> Lie, lie, lying;
> Sit, sit, sitting;
> Where will poor little carlin lie tonight?'

'You will lie behind the chest,' said the men.

> 'Beiridh biast na cist orm.
> Suidhe, suidhe, suidhegan;
> Laidhe, laidhe, laidhegan;
> Cat an caidil cailleachag, bheag bhoc?'

i.e.

'The beast of the chest will catch me.
Sit, sit, sitting;
Lie, lie, lying;
Where will poor little carlin lie to-night?'

'You will lie between ourselves, carlin,' said the men. 'That will do very well,' said the carlin, and she went over and lay among the men, seemingly much pleased.

They all went to sleep. When one of the men woke in the night he felt something warm by his side, and on putting down his hand to feel what it was he found it, to his horror, to be the clotted blood of the man who lay next to him, who lay dead by his side with a hole through his neck through which the carlin-beast had sucked his blood with her bone beak.

Site of Airidh na h-Aon Oidhche, Benbecula

an insertion by Thomas who felt that a point or two needed correction, as was certainly necessary. The 'note' began with an improbable conjecture:

Airi na h-aon Oich

'I strongly suspect that this name was originally the shieling in the wilds. Aoneach, is a lonely place – <u>Solitary.</u>

'The peculiarity of the version of the tale is in the description of the women. The bone beaks belong to creatures called Lusbairdean, if I rightly remember, which are mentioned by Martin in his Western Isles [This is a mistake; the Lusbardan of Martin are Pygmies – F W L T(homas)]. The story itself is very widely spread in Scotland. Sir Walter Scott got hold of it, and made it into Glenfinlas, in the Lady of the Lake. I think Grant Stewart has it in his 'Superstitions'. I am writing from memory so I cannot be sure of my references to these works.

'I have had the story in every possible shape from all parts of Scotland, with infinite variety of details. The exact spot is always known on which the shealing stood in which men were killed by some supernatural visitants, while one escaped by a stratagem. The story is also told in a Swedish collection of Popular tales as part of another story. The story is then a genuine bit of popular lore, which has taken root in Benbecula. Elsewhere Macphie is 'of Colonsay' (?) Elsewhere the men have other names, and their house is in Sutherland. I think the story is current in Ireland, but I cannot be sure about it.'

Campbell's reference to Scott's *The Lady of the Lake* is relevant only in that it serves to indicate that the essentials of the tale were widely known in the early years of the nineteenth century, and he was not far wrong in his recollection of a comparable story told in *The Popular Superstitions and Festive Amusements of the Highlanders of Scotland* by W Grant Stewart. This work, published in 1823, had several chapters on witchcraft, more especially one on 'their Professional Powers and Practices'. After an account of the way in which witchcraft brought about the death at sea of the Laird of Raasay, another follows with a location famed for unpleasant events – 'the forest of Gaick in Badenoch'. Here 'another hero, celebrated for his hatred of witchcraft' was sheltering in 'his hunting hut' when a witch, in the form of a cat, came in out of the storm. This was really the Wife of Laggan, who after a little while and 'assuming a most hideous and terrific appearance' sprang at the hunter. His two dogs attacked her, and she fled out of the hut, 'trailing after her the dogs, which were fastened in her so closely, that they never loosed their hold, until she demolished every tooth in their heads'. She then escaped, and the two dogs both fell dead at the hunter's feet. Soon afterwards the witch died, and her spirit, as a woman in black, was seen running for a churchyard with two large black dogs in pursuit.[11]

❖

The last of this group of four versions of the tale was taken down by Alexander Carmichael, apparently on Thursday 14 December 1871, 'from the relation of Roderick MacCarmaig, crofter, Dungaineacha, Benbecula'. Roderick could have been an immediate ancestor of Peter MacCormick. The place names and locations are more exact, and this was perhaps the outcome of Carmichael's own closer involvement.

about thirty feet high and within a few feet of the mainland.'

At most states of the tide it is possible to cross to the island, climb to the top, and sit on one of the stones in the heather there, as if in Stevenson's 'Admiral Benbow' or resting beside a road in Benbecula, contemplating the tales of MacPhee's Black Dog and Airidh na h-Aon Oidhche.

References and Notes

(Endnotes)
1. K Zickermann: 'Scottish Merchant Families in the Early Modern Period' in Northern Studies Vol.45 p.102
2. M Robson: A Sad Tale of the Sea Port of Ness 2006 pp.11, 12, 34
3. J H McCulloch: Sheep Dogs and their Masters Dumfries 1940 p.107; M Robson: St Kilda – Church, Visitors and 'Natives' Port of Ness 2005 p.722
4. See, for example, stories of Macfie's black dog related to the Island of Colonsay in John De Vere Loder: Colonsay and Oronsay In the Isles of Argyll – Their History, Flora, Fauna and Topography Edinburgh & London 1935 Chapter IX
5. For a detailed description of these sites see A S Henshall: The Chambered Tombs of Scotland Vol.II Edinburgh 1972. Airidh na h-Aon Oidhche is called (p.130) a 'curious and interesting cairn' of two-part form, comprising a roughly circular cairn and a low 'tail' of cairn material, and there is 'some indication' that it contains a burial chamber
6. A J Bruford & D A Macdonald (edits.): Scottish Traditional Tales Edinburgh 1994 pp.318-319, 470n. A tale containing rather similar events concerning the fate of the dogs was recorded from Neil Gillies, Barra, by Donald Archie MacDonald – 'Mac na Bantraich agus a Choin' (The Widow's Son and his Dogs) in Tocher no.57 pp.32-34 School of Scottish Studies, Edinburgh 2003
7. R U Sayce: 'Popular Enclosures and the One-Night House' in Montgomeryshire Collections Vol.47 (1942) pp.109-120; R U Sayce: 'The One-Night House, and its Distribution' in Folk-Lore Vol.53 (1942) pp.161-163; B. Buxton: The Vatersay Raiders Edinburgh 2008 p.89
8. Thomas Collection, Orkney Archives D3/19 (Kirkwall)
9. It is highly probable that original Gaelic versions of the 'Airidh na h-Aon Oidhche' tales are among the Carmichael Watson Papers in the Library (Special Collections) of the University of Edinburgh

Chapter VII

Scotland. What could have brought the Corncraik here so early? The weather is cold and stormy in the extreme, and as for vegetation there is none whatever; nor will there be, for the next ten weeks. Again what could have brought the Treona – Gaelic name – here so preternaturally early? I have never seen it here before June.
With warm wishes in which Mrs C joins

Yours very truly[7]

This record of the corncrake calling in March was further supported when Carmichael's children again reported hearing it at the end of the month. Its appearance so early in the season brought to mind premature occurrences of other species only a few days later, and by then Carmichael seems to be putting the first corncrake observation a week sooner than he had first noted it. His letter is undated but must have been written just after the middle of April 1882:

Dear Sir,

Just a line to say that the notice I sent you of the early appearance of the Corncreake (<u>Corncraik</u> preferable I think) has been confirmed.

Two others of our children heard the bird shortly after the eldest boy heard him about the 18th March.

Our second boy heard the bird about the end of March, or 1st April and about half a mile away from where his brother heard him.

Mr James Frazer Bank Accountant Lochmaddy while on his way here on Friday the 14th April heard the Cuckoo at Sollas N. Uist. This is abnormally early for the bleak shelterless and wood-less islands.

The first Gannet I saw this year was near this place on the 2nd April and the first Stonechat was at Carnan S. Uist on the 4th April.

Are you coming "out west" this summer? Should you come the way of Scolpaig we will be glad to see you and to give you such home fare as the place can afford.

Where is Capt. Fielden?

Yours very truly

However domestically established at Scolpaig this letter may sound, Carmichael had scanty financial resources and somehow failed to retain his hold on the land where his greatest work had been accomplished. In 1883 he uprooted himself and family once again and went to Edinburgh where he resided for several years at 31 Raeburn Place.[8] By this time Harvie-Brown had started to work on his proposed account of the wild life of the Outer Hebrides and made visits to many of the more remote islands in his yacht. In the summer of 1885 he reached Rona, forty miles north-east of Lewis, where a few months earlier the remains of two Ness men and their abandoned dwelling had been found. This discovery aroused considerable public interest and after exhumation a post mortem was carried out at the end of May, followed immediately by a re-burial in the little cemetery. Two weeks later Harvie-Brown arrived and concentrated on observing birds and their nesting, but he was, as all who go to Rona, fascinated by the story of the island and its former inhabitants. So too was Alexander Carmichael, and the two men corresponded on the then rather mysterious episode of the fate of Malcolm Macdonald and Murdo Mackay. Two of

Chapter VII

'My dear Mr. Carmichael

You astonish me about Ferguson: and yet do you know that I was puzzled a good deal when reviewing his papers in the Trans. of the Gaelic Soc. of Inverness, as to how he – a common gardener – and a young man still – a native of Mid-Perthshire, where even land birds are scarce, and sea birds of course unknown – how he could have got the Gaelic names of so many birds of land and sea: <u>and all so correctly</u>, and with such a store of folk-lore illustrative.

    Believing him however to be all right, I praised him very highly, and advised him to rewrite the whole, to add and improve in various ways, and to publish in booklet form a volume which should be a fitting companion to Camerons Gaelic names of Plants.

    Fergusson wrote to me thanking me for my review and advice, and assuring me that he was already engaged at the papers, and meant to publish them at once in book form as suggested.

    I don't wonder at your being annoyed and I do think he deserves to be exposed. But how did you happen to let the fellow get your papers at all? It is not one man in a thousand that I would lend any papers of mine, upon which I set the least value; unless indeed I meant to make him a present of it, and the understanding that he might do with it what he liked. I cannot now remember the date of my paper on the Gaelic Transactions, but if you drop a note to Mr. Barron Editor of the Courier, he will find it for you and send you a copy, or Mr. Wm. Mackay could easily manage it for you.'

On 31 March 1887 Carmichael immediately wrote to Harvie-Brown, taking up initially the more welcome subject of his writings on Rona and then returning to the Fergusson issue:

Dear Sir,

I have to thank you very warmly for your courteous and considerate letter together with the Roney papers.

[Just now?] I have time only to say that your papers are always of great interest to me. I do not know that there is any man in Scotland who deserves more praise, if so much, as you do for your indefatigable exertions in the cause of natural history, and that too in so many departments of it.

As I mentioned to you, Mr William Mackay Inverness is strongly urging me not to let Ferguson pass. I sent him the sheets which I lent to Ferguson so that he might see for himself how the matter stands. When I get the sheets back I will send them to you and you will be better able to judge of Ferguson's cool impertinence to say no worse.

"Nether Lochaber" reviewed the Gaelic bird names in the <u>Courier</u> and I wrote asking him the date of his review. I enclose you his letter from which you will see that he too had his doubts about Ferguson. Again thanking you

Yours very truly

P.S. The allusion to our boy is his having been elected to a Fettes College Foundation through the interest of quite a large number of the foremost men in Edinburgh. These interested themselves in behalf of our boy in a manner which we can never forget. A.C.

Chapter VII

I think the Gaelic Society Transactions will be good this year. Mr William Mackay who is in charge this year told me that he was resolved that they should be so.

Two of our boys leave on Thursday on an Easter holiday visit to Mr Dixon, Inveran, who with more than kindness has already paid all their expenses! We hardly know what to say. When these boys return, if not before, I will avail myself of your kind invitation and come to see 1st yourself, 2nd your wonderful collection.

If not inconvenient to you I will go on a Saturday and come back on a Monday.

Yours very truly

P.S. I wish you would do us the pleasure of coming down to see us when you are in town. Drop us a post card so that we may not be out. A.C.

❖

So far as his communication with Harvie-Brown was concerned Carmichael returned at this stage to the matter of listing birds. Harvie-Brown was busy preparing material not only on birds but also on animals and fishes for his Outer Hebrides book, of which the nominal authorship at least he shared with T E Buckley. Questions and answers, comments and observations, again passed to and fro, mixed with Carmichael's feelings as he let his mind range over all sorts of associated thoughts and concerns. His letter of 15 April is typical in this respect:

Alexander Carmichael writes to John A Harvie-Brown

Dear Sir,

Your scathing criticism is to hand and if it applied to me I would immediately go and hang myself.

When I began to take down the Gaelic names of birds it was [simply?] from a mere love – a sort of instinct, or passion with me, to take down all old Gaelic things to rescue them from being lost! I saw old habits and customs, names of birds, beasts, and places dying out rapidly and I wished to rescue what I could. That was all. I think it was Capt. Elwes who first asked me to give him the Gaelic names of birds, and this led me to look into long laid aside scraps, - books, and string together as many of the names as I could lay my hands on.

Several other gentlemen visitors to Uist asked me for the Gaelic names and I was always delighted to give them what I had, though I never made any pretence to accuracy or fullness. The list handed to Ferguson were the [loose?] sheets from which I made <u>the lists</u> for friends from time to time – always a delight to me.

I often thought, however, in my own mind that I would like to make out a <u>correct</u> list – and mine made no pretence to correctness – of all the Gaelic names of birds, together with any proverbs or old sayings about birds, and then have the whole revised <u>thoroughly</u> and [?] by one or more scientific ornithologists: My ambition did not go beyond the Gaelic names, and their accretions – For example –

"Nead air Bhrid, ubh air Inid, ian air Chasg;
Mur bith sid aig an t-sean fhitheach bithidh am bas"

Chapter VII

[Literal translation?] -
Nest at Saint Brid's (1 Feb.), egg at Shrovetide, and chick at Easter, if the <u>old</u> raven has not these, he has death.

This is an example of what I meant; but of course there is no knowing how far my conceit or want of knowledge might lead me had not another taken the wind of my sails! I thought, and still think, and feel an accurate Gaelic list of bird-names and old Gaelic sayings and rhymes about birds, would be interesting to men living in the future when Gaelic and Gaelic names are dead. Unluckily for myself, however, my heart is only full of good intentions and [the?] my head of sentiment and the bird-names in Gaelic like scores of similar things of mine are undone by me.
Many thanks for all your trouble.

Yours very truly

The main point was pursued further on 20 April 1887:

Dear Sir,

I have just been looking over your list of fishes for the third or fourth time. I can give the names of a good many of these in Gaelic better. The difficulty with me is under which particular name to place the Gaelic name there being so many different kinds. If you would permit me I would like to send copies to two or three men in the Isles who know these fishes and their Gaelic names better than I do. You are doing noble work and it would be a shame if [Every?] Highlander did not do his best to help you to record the Gaelic names, so fast dying out.

I have <u>many</u> hundred of Gaelic names of beasts and birds and reptiles Grasses trees and shrubs and of fishes and shellfishes scattered over my scrap books. But the difficulty is where to look for a single name when I want it. If I had only time to arrange and systematise these [?] confused scrap-books and think a good deal of interesting and in some cases useful information could be got from them.
There is not hurry at all for the bird sheets.

Yours very truly

The next surviving letter in the collection (2 August 1887), rather more familiar in tone, told a seal story, seals naturally being part of Harvie-Brown's 'Fauna':

My Dear Mr Harvie-Brown

Just a line. This evening while searching for information about birds beasts reptiles and fishes, I was told that there used to be a seal on Sgeir-nam-Maol nowhere else to be seen round all the coast. This seal is said to have the upper jaw curving down over the under jaw, much like the beak of a bird of prey. The head is long, and large.

Sgeir-nam-Maol lies off the north end of Skye. There is a perch on the rock now and the seal is seldom seen since this perch was placed there. Before then many of these seals used to be seen on this rock. So it is told me. I write you this bit of information – if information it be – to you, lest you may be able to make use of it ere you return home.

My intelligent informant says that one seal of this kind was seen in the sea between Scalpey and Raasey.

Chapter VII

I refrain from bothering you with more till you come home. When you do I may bother you with much – perhaps too much of my "wares". I hope you are [enjoying?] yourself greatly.

Wishing you all enjoyment and happiness
Yours very sincerely

After another gap of three months, in the course of which Harvie-Brown must have sent Carmichael one of John Finlayson's accounts of birds and social life on the island of Mingulay, south of Barra, the paper was returned with a short reminiscence on 8 November 1887. Finlayson was a Free Church teacher among the Catholic population, married a girl of the island, and stayed there for most of the rest of his life. He was evidently one of the best of Harvie-Brown's informants and Carmichael had met him on his own visits to 'Miulaidh', or 'Miuley' as he rendered the Gaelic name.

Dear Mr Harvie-Brown,

I return you Finlayson's paper with an explanation scribbled on the back. The paper is interesting.

I know Finlayson well and have known him for a quarter of a century. He is a decent intelligent fellow and could he have been got to write down all that he knew and all that he could find out about his island he could have put together most interesting things. I often urged this upon him. He and old men there told me many interesting things, principally about birds and fishes. These I noted down. The difficulty is to get at them now.

The late Mr Campbell of Islay and I were three nights storm stayed in Miuley in Oct. 1872. We were quite happy.

> Mr Campbell was one of the noblest natured men I ever knew or hope to know. I had a warm love for him which was returned.
>
> Lord Lorne came to see us here the other day. He made himself most condescending and pleasant and said that Mrs C – and myself were "familiar to him through his kinsman Ian Campbell". In leaving after a long visit he said that he hoped he would "see us in his house". That was very kind and condescending of him wasn't it?
>
> You do not say how you feel or how your venerable and honoured mother is?
>
> Yours very truly[12]

Late in 1887 Harvie-Brown was looking for engravings or photographs of William MacGillivray, who was appointed Professor of Civil and Natural History at Aberdeen in 1841, and his son John MacGillivray, to use as illustrations in his forthcoming book. He eventually discovered one picture of each, but in his letter of 30 November 1887 Carmichael, who had been asked if he could find any, said that he was then still looking for them:

> Dear Mr Harvie Brown,
>
> I omitted to say that I do not know where to procure a likeness of the MacGillivrays either of father or son. I do not think that the MacGillivrays Barra have any but I will write and see. I will also write Mrs Paterson Bearnaray, Sound of Harris and see if she has any or if she can direct me. She lived for several years with her cousin the professor at Aberdeen.

Chapter VII

She told me a good many things of great interest about her cousin and also about Audubon who stayed much at the Professors. I noted down many of these interesting statements. I wish I had now time to look them up.

I began last night to look over my scrapbooks all in the rough as taken down to see what I could come across in the ways of notes on birds and animals. I find that many of the weird tales I took down contain highly interesting things in prose and rhyme about animals. Oh! how I wish I could live without the hateful – to me always hateful – Excise Service and so have time to arrange these things!

You are all keeping better I am glad to hear from Dr. Carmichael.

Yours very truly

It may have been that Carmichael was already feeling fairly gloomy again, and not only because of his excise work, when at about this time he sent some notes on birds to Harvie-Brown. They were numbered as follows, aroused responses, and were followed by further information which culminated in some of the most telling sentences which Carmichael ever wrote:

I

Somewhere, probably in Islay, the Pipit is called Uiseag; so probably Uiseag Choille is the Tree Pipit as you suggest. Uiseag Choille is a term applied in Uist also.

II

Uiseag Cladaich, literally shore-lark is no doubt the Shore Pipit or Rock Pipit.

III

You see what blunders slovenly writing causes. You mistake my C in Clisgein for F. The name is Clisgein from clisg swift, and ian bird – the swift bird "Cho clisg ris a Chlisgein" – its swift as the Swift-bird – applied to a person whose actions are very quick and ceaseless, like those of Kay of the <u>Dunara</u> for example.

IV

I will send you a Note such as you ask for.

V

I meant Iolair Cladaich, Shore Eagle, for the Sea Eagle and not the Golden Eagle.

VI

My own opinion is that Lainnir is meant to apply to the bravery of the bird. In my native island of Lismore – the only place by the way in which the phrase is ever used – I often heard "Is tu an lann", thou art the <u>lann</u> applied to a brave boy who performed a brave clever action. Lann I take it is the root of Lannair or Lainnir as applied to the Peregrine Falcon. The dictionaries give "Lannair (from Lann) Radiance; Glitter; Splendour; a gleaming light reflected on the blade of a sword or any burnished metal surface.

VII

The well and often [tried?] sword of Iain mac Iain 'ic Sheumais, a well known warrior of the Western Isles, who led and successfully the Macdonalds against the Macleods at the battle of Cairnish in North Uist in 1601 was called by some, an Rannaire Riabhach, the brindled rhymer and by others the Lannaire Riabhach. I take it means "the brindled Gleamer or something of that sort. Lannair and Lainnir mean the same thing. My own opinion is that the name Lainnir for the

Chapter VII

I

Note by J.A.H-B

'But the true Woodlark is unknown or almost unknown in Scotland. Harvie-Brown took the only recorded nest of the species. It is a S. Eastern Counties species – Norfolk Cambridge etc. Is <u>Uiseag choille</u> not applied to a <u>Tree pipit</u> or to some other bird of the wood?'

II

'Also Shore Lark (119) (Otocorip.) is <u>not</u> British breeding species. No doubt "Uiseag chladaich" is applied to the Rock pipit (68) as well as its other names Uiseag dubh (& Bigean mor = Corn bunting).'

III

'Swift (132) Cypselus apus. I cannot quite make out these Gaelic names in correct spelling.

Is <u>An flisgein</u> correct? and 'Cho des ris fhlisgein' – [Carmichael seems to have written 'Cho clisg ris a fhlisgein' - See III above]

IV

'Could you give me a little explanatory sentence about the grammar and spelling which could appear in a Foot-note or paragraph in Introduction – I mean as to gender thus An *flisgein* and *fhlisgein* & so on helping to explain what to Southern eyes appear irregularities – mor & mohr etc.'

V

'Under Golden Eagle

I have Iolair cladaich & you add the note = "Shore-Eagle, but (query) is this name not more correctly applied to the white-tailed or Sea-Eagle?'

VI

'Peregrine falcon. I cannot quite make out the possible translation of lainnir – "might be translated the gleaming ? (sword?) or "lance"?, in allusion to the colour of the bird (i.e. blue like steel?) & the "rarity" (?) of the bird. Please say.
JAHB
Note. It is curious to find a closely allied form in Egypt called Lanner Falcon.'

'Falco subbuteo L Hobby
Gaelic Obag: Gormag = the little blue one.
Now the Hobby is very <u>rare</u> in Scotland. Yet I presume it was more abundant at one time. I myself have seen it in the Black Wood of Rannoch. It is like a miniature Peregrine Falcon
The <u>Merlin</u> is still common.
Query. Were these two distinctly separated by Gaelic names?

<u>Comments [on the above Harvie-Brown notes] by Alexander Carmichael</u>

I am not a naturalist – only a lover of nature and a recorder of the Gaelic names of birds animals and fishes etc and desirous nay [?] anxious to do everything in my power to help others more happily situated than myself in placing on record everything connected with my beloved Highlands and Islands whether it be as to their peoples, their language, their antiquities, or their natural history.

My Gaelic names include not only the birds of the Outer Hebrides but those of whatever place for which I can procure Gaelic names.

Invariably the observant old people from whom I get the old names, runs, and rhymes have no knowledge whatever of the corresponding English name of the birds etc whose Gaelic name they give me. When I also do not know the English name I note down a description of the birds as given me by the old people. And after all I often find it difficult sometimes impossible to classify the bird under its correct English name much as I puzzle over it.

I have no high opinion of Gray's <u>Birds of the West of Scotland</u> *but I believe the following quotations are correct:- "In the O Hebrids the Chiffchaff frequents Rhodil in Haris as I have been informed by Mr Elwes who procured a specimen in May 1868. Mr Brown informs me that it breeds in Dunmore woods Stirling there and that he has seen its nest taken by Mr Thompson who believes that it nests there regularly." Gray p.98*

I think the Chiffchaff is in the woods around Stornoway Castle.

Ceann-dearg = red-head; Ceann-deargan = "little red-head". I rather think I ought to have placed this name opposite the Goldfinch and not opposite the Redstart.

Caifein = "the little chaffer" (bird). Caifein is also applied to a dog that barks weakly and ceaselessly as "[Cuilt?] a chaifean" "Whist! Thou chafferer"! Caifein Coille – "the woodchaffer or chafferer".

Cuilcein = "the little reedling bird" from <u>cuilc</u> reed and <u>ein</u> the oblique form of <u>ian</u>, bird.

<u>Ceolan</u> = dim. of <u>ceol</u>, music. I rather think the name is <u>Ceoilein</u> the musical little bird. <u>Ceolan</u> or <u>Ceoilein Cuilce</u> "the

little musical bird of the reeds". From want of knowing better, I placed the name opposite the Reed Warbler – wrongly it would appear.

Bricein Buidhe dim. of *breac* speckled and *buidhe* yellow. "the little yellow speckley [?] Is this another name for the Yellow Hammer – the Yellow Yeorling?

"*Am Bricein Buidhe boidheach*
Air oireadh na greine
Caideidl e na sheomar
Am mhoiead na streupa"

The bonnie yellow birdling
Like the sunny summer beams
He sleeps in his chamber
Though great be the battle (of the winds)

Cnag = a rap, a knock; a pin, as, a [thole?] pin; a tree stump etc.

In conclusion I am rather inclined to give up the thankless task of collecting the Gaelic names, traditions, superstitions, proverbs and rhymes and runs about birds, beasts, reptiles, insects, fishes, and shell-fishes. It is rather disheartening to a man like myself who impoverished himself in rescuing what he could of the rapidly dying out oral literature of his native countrymen, and not only impoverished himself, but declined promotion most kindly offered to him several times – it is rather disheart[en]ing I say, to find so much filching of the results of his labours among so many of his fellow countrymen and that without the slightest indication of their source.

Chapter VII

I could tell you many curious cases and that at the hands of some men of whom you would not expect it and who have never done anything themselves except to study their own dear interest. I sometimes feel so disheartened as to be inclined to throw my whole gathering of some thirty years work into the fire and be done with it!

A. Carmichael
Edinburgh
3.12.1887

❖

But fortunately Carmichael roused himself from this state of what seemed to be deep depression. The dominating interest for both Harvie-Brown and Carmichael towards the end of 1887 and during most of 1888 was again the Gaelic names of birds, though on occasion other vertebrate creatures made similar claims on their attention. Most of Carmichael's letters therefore from that of 5 December 1887 to those in the autumn of the following year were written with the approaching publication of Harvie-Brown's Outer Hebrides book looming ever larger in the background. One of the ornithological problems they had was caused by the variety of possible Gaelic names for one and the same species and consequently the difficulty of identification when translating into another language. Much could depend on making a choice between usages in different islands, as Carmichael pointed out in his 5 December letter:

Dear Mr Harvie Brown,

The bird and fish names are often as perplexing to me as they can possibly be to you and they sometimes make me despair of making anything satisfactory of my self imposed task.
As I said to you already I get names Gaelic names of course and neither any informant or myself know the corresponding English name. In such a case I make the best attempt, perhaps I should say, the best guess I can. Take these for example.
In Islay the Skylark is called the Reamhag – that is the Riabhag the name applied in Lismore to the Meadow Pipit. In Uist the Raven is Fitheach; in Harris Biatach; In Uist the grey Crow is called Feannag; in Harris Starrag. Many other examples could be mentioned making it exceedingly difficult for a simple lover of nature and not a naturalist to un[ra]vel the tangled skein of Gaelic names.

   Before sending in your list to the printer I would like to go over the Gaelic names [etc.?]

   The obliquities and aspirations in Gaelic are a source of trouble to strangers, sometimes to natives; but never to the uneducated natives. No; that is the curious thing in Gaelic grammar that those wholly unacquainted with grammar invariably speak the language grammatically.

Yours very truly

There followed a lone sheet, with the date 27 January 1888, which must have been part of another, missing letter. What is left contains only:

Chapter VII

Donald Lamont is angry at such an incredible absurdity being attributed to him as that he could see, even were he living in sight of the Minch, whereas he is not a direct distance of say from fifteen to twenty miles! In short, I look upon Mr Grays <u>Birds of the West of Scotland</u> as a piece of down right impudence – an imposition. Others do the same.

In looking over your proof again I see that not only have several of the Gaelic names got displaced but that many are omitted altogether.

I sent my bird list long ago to Newton to see if he could add to it. I will write for it again and then do all I can for your proof. I will see Mr Douglas.

As this letter is already too long I will say Goodbye asking you at the same time to forgive all I have said about the late Mr Gray.

Yours very truly

P.S. As you are writing about the birds of the west I thought it was only right of me to tell you honestly my opinion of Grays book. I was there during his visits, saw him each time and saw what he did or rather what he did not. He speaks of what he saw in South Uist. I believe I do not injustice to Mr Gray in saying that he never was in South Uist or in Barra or in Harris or in the island of Lewis. He was two or three at Stornoway just for a day or so at a time. A.C.

In all this correspondence Carmichael conveys the impression that he is seeking to overcome a sense of inferiority by ingratiating himself with some, especially with Harvie-Brown himself, and by disparaging others. There was really no need for him to do either, but perhaps as an excise employee he felt out of his depth when straying outside the limits of his work into natural history of any kind and perhaps even into folklore. He did not leave Gray alone with his letter of 10 April but took up the subject again in another only two days later, in which he records a meeting with 'Mr Constable', presumably one of the publishing firm of T & A Constable which eventually produced the first two volumes of Carmichael's own collections.

Dear Harvie-Brown

On my return a few minutes ago from my visit to Mr Constable I found your letter in before me.

I found Mr Constable very nice indeed and we soon became warm friends, when he discovered that I was on friendly terms with his uncles and aunts the Cowans and Mr Colin Macvean.

Mr Constable is to write you and he will give me what you suggest and so save time.

You will pardon me for speaking so freely about Mr Gray's book. I felt and still feel however that your own book would be more or less compromised by quoting Gray as an authority.

What would you think of yourself or of me if you or I landed at Lochmaddy early in the morning say on the arrival of the steamer from Glasgow and then perhaps in the course of an hour or two start for Nunton in Benbecula; inspect the books of the bank there, and back again the following day. And then after either two or at most three hurried runs of this description to Nunton and the same to Stornoway write about the birds of the Long Island! Would you not say that you or I or indeed any one who did this was guilty of down right

Chapter VII

impudence? You who know those interesting islands well know how difficult it is to ascertain their ornithology even after you have travelled over the whole length and breadth of them.

I saw Mr Norman Macdonald of the bank a good deal before he left for Australia in Nov. last. We had several talks about Gray and his book. Norman's opinion was that either Gray was short sighted or that his knowledge of birds was very unequal to his pretentions.

On several occasions in driving him back to Lochmaddy he asked Norman the names of birds they saw, and when he named birds himself he was as often wrong as he was right. Norman is a shrewd observant fellow who has an excellent knowledge of the birds and beasts of Uist without any pretentions to be a naturalist. Unlike Gray again Macgillivray took infinite pains with his birds. The old people speak of how he constructed places of concealment where to watch the Eagle, the Tarmigan and other mountain birds in their breeding haunts and how he was wont to go up to those "conceals" at night in order to watch their morning movements and how in some of those "conceals" he remained for six weeks at a time – often drenched for days and nights often nearly frozen to death and invariably nearly dead from hunger.

It was a miracle to many how he lived or survived his mountain pilgrimages. The result is that apart altogether from my admiration of his writings I feel a profound admiration bordering on worship for MacGillivray but for Gray's pretentions I candidly confess I feel nothing but contempt.

A parcel is just come from Constable.

Oh! How I wish my time were my own to devote to this and kindred pursuits.

Yours very truly'[14]

❖

As the day of the publication of Harvie-Brown's book drew closer Carmichael's letters became more varied with comments on unexpected subjects interspersed among the information on birds, usually within the letters but occasionally on separate sheets. For instance, his letter of 13 April 1888 was accompanied by a commentary on dogs and their names.

Dear Harvie-Brown,

As my bird list has not yet arrived from Newton to whom I sent it for any additional Gaelic names he could give me, I send you the proof you sent me some days ago as it is. When my own list comes I will be able to add some more Gaelic names.

I have to apologise to you for writing notes on your proof. If you disapprove of them please draw your pen through them.

Mr Constable sent me a large pile of proofs last night. I have looked over these sheets and find that there is a good deal to do to some of them but to others happily not much. I will do all I can to them and as soon as I can. But as these are things that need much care at least I feel so, I cannot hurry them out of hand. When a man has several irons in the fire and can only attend to them intermittently I fear the result is never satisfactory to himself or to others. But so it is and we must just submit to the collar as well as we can!

Yours very truly[15]

Chapter VII

The commentary on dogs of the same date and signed by Alexander Carmichael seems to follow an extract from a Journal, probably by Harvie-Brown:

'Mr Mcdonalds active little terriers – (1) Fionnag (a mite) (2) Cullag (a flea) & (3) Garry (an otters Cairn) – the Corncrakes at Newton have a lively time of it. I would that there is a breath of wind <u>any day</u> back Fionnag & Cullag to put up every Corncrake in the meadow – and they are not few.'

> (1) *Fianag* = mite; (2) *Cuilleag* = fly; (3) *Garraidh* = otter cairn
>
> *Note – Garraidh was the most rascally dog I ever saw. He was a wiry wiry-haired, black and some what [brown?] terrier of extraordinary courage, grip and tenacity. No dog however big had a chance with him. He went straight at any big dog that came the way no matter how big and powerful. He fought on his back just as well as on his legs. He could not reach up to the body of a big dog but he went at his legs and drove his fangs right through them. The result was that all the big dogs about the place during Garraidh's long reign had but sorry times of it! All the dogs of the cowherds and shepherds of the farm had a wholesome hon[?] of Garraidh! And no wonder. You saw them limping and hobbling about – sometimes on three sometimes on two legs and sometimes with hardly a leg at all under them. When you asked the owner as sometimes wicke[dly you] did what was the matter with his dog the answer invariably was "That d --- d <u>Garraidh</u> has been at him again"! Strange dogs which had been over at Newton never liked to go back there again. I have seen the poor fellows stopping short and sitting on a knoll within sight and sound of the house and then waiting and watching*

till their master came back rather than go down to Newton house.

Garraidh had hardly a whole bit of bone in his body or a whole patch of skin on his back; and even then fought as one of the shepherds said as if he were possessed of the devils and not like any christian dog! Poor Garraidh became so horribly maimed and disfigured and so repugnant and abhorrant to all the dogs of the farm and their masters that he had at last to be killed.

Poor fellow he was a splendid dog – a warm friend of man though a furious enemy to his own species, to otters, rats, cats, and pigs.'

The next letter, of 3 July 1888, was back to a more regular level, with yet another slant at Gray:

Dear Mr Harvie-Brown,

The book you were sending has not come. I hope it is not yet sent lest it is lost.

Did I tell you that Newton and Ferguson Lochboisdale sent me back the Bird List and Fish list which I sent to them for additions and correction and after retaining them for half a year without a *single* addition, without a *single* correction? I felt very much hurt and do still. These are men for whom I would put myself about to any conceivable extent and happy in the doing it if thereby I could only oblige them even in the smallest. They are moreover men who could help in these names as no other two men in the Highlands could. It shows what little, what *very little*, interest or enthusiasm you can infuse in people about things which you may have deeply at heart.

Chapter VII

> *Ferguson came up to town in hot haste about a prosecution pending over the fishermen for fishing lobsters during the close time. I went with him to several places for the old Act on the subject G.II, c.35. We could not get it anywhere and he had to leave. I found the Act in the Register House copied it and sent it after him.*
>
> *I had peculiar satisfaction in copying that old Act of Parliament for Ferguson and that just a few days after getting back my Fish List from Ferguson without a single addition without a single correct! Don't think me malicious! Perhaps I told you all this before? I am so forgetful.*
>
> *I hope your venerable mother is keeping better. I have not been able to see my namesake for some time to ask him. When in town could you not do us the honour of coming to see us? You might send a post card, and I would make a point of being in.*
>
> *I did not mean to touch your [?] again. I did so to draw your eye to what I thought wrong. Gray simply humbugged the ornithologists with his book and I am sorry you rely on his utterly unreliable statements. Two runs of a day or run each to Benbecula and Stornoway could hardly entitle any <u>modest, honourable</u> man to write a book on the birds of the Outer Hebrides. I have no patience with humbugs!*
>
> *Yours very truly*[16]

The letter of 31 October deals with 'reptiles' or 'serpents', neither of which, in spite of certain local information, seem to have existed in the Outer Hebrides, although Harvie-Brown briefly mentioned them in his book.

Dear Mr Harvie Brown,

It so happens that I never saw a reptile in the Outer Hebrides. The late Mr Donald Macdonald, Keallann, told me that the Lizard is at Keallann, in Grimisey North Uist and that he saw it there. I have no reason to disbelieve Mr Macdonald's statement; but I never saw a Lizard there. There is this difference however that although I was often at Keallann I was not living there and Mr Macdonald was for many years, that being his farm.

I am not yet satisfied that the "serpent" in Harris and Lewis is other than the Slowworm. I saw the mangled remains of one or two but they were so far gone that I could not make out what they were.

The people both in Harris and Lewis assured me that they had the real serpent there as they had good cause to know from their Lewis cattle and sheep getting stung by the serpent and they related many examples.

I am sorry to write to so little purpose.

Yours very truly[17]

One of the few 'mammals' on which Carmichael wrote to Harvie-Brown was the black rat, for which he felt some affection as he said in his letter of 2 November 1888:

Dear Mr Harvie Brown,

The only two places at which I have ever seen the Black Rat are Creagorry and Gramsdail – both in Benbecula. My special acquaintance with it extended from 1872 to 1879 during which time we lived in Benbecula. Among the many

Chapter VII

follies of which we were guilty when living at Creagorry we built a wing to the back of the house. There was a separate entrance to our house by this wing. There was a foot scraper at the door and in order to have it out of the way I got the mason to make a recess for it in the wall of the old house – not the wing. I do not know how but the Black Rat manage[d] to discover or to make a passage in this miniature cave wherein the door scraper was recessed. I think there would be two or three or so of Black Rats quietly slipping out and in now and again here. Mrs Carmichael who as you know is very observant and who takes a very intelligent interest in all these things saw these Black Rats repeatedly. She and I liked to see the glossy black beautiful creatures and we gave strict injunctions to the servants not to molest upon any account but rather to treat them kindly. The pretty creatures seemed to feel as if they were among friends. At any rate it was our sincere desire that they should so feel and feel at home and they were never injured. Whether they are there still or not I cannot say. Probably not, the people who are there now are wiser than to bother prudent heads or hearts about sentiment or about Rats Black or Brown – British or Hanoverian, Stewart or Guelph. We have an old Gaelic saying which alas, I have never observed – **Togaidh an Goraiche an caisteal is gabhaidh an gliocaire comhnuidh ann** *– The foolish (man) builds the castle and the wise (man) dwells in it. Probably the Black Rat of Creagorry has been singing if in a singing mood Pitcairn's lines to Montrose –*

    "New people fill the Land now ye are gone
    New gods the temple and new Kings the throne"
    Pray excuse all this – probably the [undertone?] of a foolish heart rather than the language of a wise head.

*As already mentioned the only other place at which I ever saw the Black Rat was at Gramsdail on north east strand of the island of Benbecula – directly opposite Creagorry which is on the South West strand. And even then I did not see the rat in the flesh – only the skin. The skin was on the road in front of the frightfully tumble down crazy little inn. I lifted up the skin – it was still warm after the iniquitous operations of a cat probably. The skin was beautifully flayed and beautifully glossy. A gentleman who was along with me asked me what it was. I told him. he said that he would like to keep the skin for a **spleucan**, tobacco pouch and he kept it and probably he has it still. Mrs Macdonald of the little inn and now of Manitoba told me that they occasionally saw the Black Rat, not in the house, but about the place.*

That is all that I can say about the Black Rat – many words but little substance.

There is no water near the old inn at Gramsdail except the sea which comes up the door at high water. Neither is there water near our old house at Creagorry except the salt water of the Atlantic which comes within fifty yards or so of the back of the house.

The Brown Rat is numerous enough and destructive enough in Benbecula. We were not much bothered but down at the old inn where there is a jetty for landing meal flour and other goods the Brown Rat followed out his Hanoverian instincts to the full – he increased and multiplied and propagated his kind after the manner of his kind and country men and lived on the fat of the land and sea. He came in for a good deal of abuse and hard names – abuse that no highminded four-footed or two footed rat would or could stand but he heeded not, no, not he. He went on as before – followed

Chapter VII

surprisingly there was no mention of birds. They remarked, in respect of fieldfares (p.46), that Carmichael had seen them on 'Haskeir' in mid October 1878, when probably he was there to see the seals. And in their account of deer they acknowledged Carmichael's note as the only information they had about the name of one of Barra's accompanying, lesser islands:

'The rough high island of Maoldonuich, at the entrance to Castlebay or Macneillton, is known to the old people as Eilean-nam-Fiadh, the island of the deer, because of deer kept there by the old Macneills of Barray. The better known name of Maoldonuich , Saint Dominus, is after one of the early Celtic saints who had his cell there. – *Note by Alexander Carmichael.*'

A dozen years after <u>A Vertebrate Fauna</u> appeared the first two volumes of Carmichael's <u>Carmina Gadelica</u> were published, and on 7 November 1901 Carmichael wrote the last of his letters to Harvie-Brown, or at any rate the last to survive in the collection. He was now living at another Edinburgh address, 37 Polwarth Gardens:

Dear Mr Harvie Brown,

I have been from home or I would have written you before now. It was to me most disappointing not to have seen you when I called.

Yes, I would be very pleased indeed to have an opportunity of revising the Gaelic names for it is anything but comforting to see errors above your initials.

My wife and I spent the month of June in Barra. I saw Finlayson who spoke well of you and of your work.

There's but little doing in birds in Barra now. The only thing that I read of or saw was William MacGillivray's collection. That collection is very good and very interesting. I urged upon William to put on the Gaelic names or names of each bird and when shot. I hope he will.

I am busy at the third volume of the <u>Old Hymns</u> and hope to have some more things to say about birds and seals and fishes then. The rhymes already given seem to interest readers.

I suppose like myself you are busy and I must not farther intrude.

Yours very truly

So, with another visit to Barra and preparation of a third volume of <u>Carmina Gadelica</u> the present story ends.

Chapter VII

References and Notes

(Endnotes)

1. Consideration of Alexander Carmichael's interest in birds is provided by Tristan Ap Rheinalt in <u>A Thankless Task ? Alexander Carmichael as a collector of Gaelic bird names</u> South Lochs, Isle of Lewis 2010
2. D U Stiùbhart: <u>The Life and Legacy of Alexander Carmichael</u> Isle of Lewis 2008 p.5. This book is a most useful guide to Carmichael's life and work
3. R Gray: <u>The Birds of the West of Scotland including The Outer Hebrides</u> Glasgow 1871 pp.11-12. In due course Harvie-Brown briefly told this story without mentioning either Gray or Carmichael as his source (Harvie-Brown & Buckley: <u>A Vertebrate Fauna of the Outer Hebrides</u> Edinburgh 1888 p.84): 'Dr. MacGillivray of Eoligary, Barray, had a tame White-tailed Eagle for some time, and this bird used to follow his sons in their rambles over the island'
4. R Gray: <u>The Birds of the West of Scotland including The Outer Hebrides</u> Glasgow 1871 pp.28, 349-350, 368, 408, 422, and 329
5. John Francis Campbell (of Islay) had composed <u>Frost and Fire: natural engines, tool-marks and chips: with sketches taken at home and abroad by a traveller</u> about 1865, in which year it was published by Edmonston and Douglas (Edinburgh: R Clark). Carmichael had met the author about five years earlier, a meeting which did much to launch Carmichael on his pursuits of folklore. Harvie-Brown set off from Granton (Edinburgh) for Norway with his friend Edward Alston, another keen naturalist and author, on 5 May 1871, but does not seem to have had time or the inclination to have followed up Carmichael's suggestion [See J A Harvie-Brown: <u>Travels of a Naturalist in Northern Europe</u> London 1895 Vol.1 p.3]

    The postscript to Carmichael's letter has been pasted over with a slip of paper so that it is only partially legible

6. Pencil note presumably by Harvie-Brown: original bound in H-B's "commonplace Book A to S Vol.I" p.145

7 Note by Harvie-Brown: 'Entered in MS but reserved for further consideration.' It seems that Harvie-Brown decided to change the corncrake of the letter into a cuckoo. The entry in A Vertebrate Fauna of the Outer Hebrides (p.76) was: 'It is not at all clear that the Cuckoo never remains in the Hebrides all winter, as authentic accounts are extant of its occurrences as early as March 25, 1882 (Alexander Carmichael, in lit. 27th March 1882), and we have similar accounts from other favoured island localities.' However, it appears that the same letter, in which there is no mention of a cuckoo, was, rather freely, quoted as evidence of the early arrival of the corncrake! (Harvie-Brown & Buckley 1888 p.122)

8 It has been said recently that Carmichael and family left for Edinburgh in the summer of 1882 (D U Stiùbhart 2008 p.15) and this may be the correct year, but Harvie-Brown & Buckley (1888 p.29) in giving the number of deer in Harris according to Martin Martin as 'at least 2000' also quoted a note by Alexander Carmichael in confirmation: 'This was the computed number of deer in Harris when I left the Outer Hebrides in 1883

9 For further information on Rona, the fate of the two men living there in 1884/5, and the 'calendar', see M Robson: Rona – the Distant Island Stornoway 1991, and A Sad Tale of the Sea – The story of Malcolm MacDonald and Murdo MacKay on the Island of Rona Port of Ness 2006

10 It seems likely that the paper sent by Carmichael was an item now preserved in the Carmichael Watson Collection, University of Edinburgh Library [CWC 230]. Harvie-Brown's paper is probably: 'Further Notes on North Rona, being an Appendix to Mr John Swinburn's Paper on that Island in the "Proceedings" of this Society, 1883-84' in Proceedings of the Royal Physical Society of Edinburgh 1885-88 pp.284-89. It is worth noting that Harvie-Brown, who visited Rona in 1885 and again in 1887, composed a lengthy introduction to the island for A Vertebrate Fauna of the Outer Hebrides largely based on quotations from other authors and from his own journals but not from Alexander Carmichael's papers

11 For the two parts of Charles Fergusson's papers on 'The Gaelic Names of Birds' see TGSI Vol.XI pp.240-260 and Vol.XII pp.28-93

12 All pages of this letter were deleted with a vertical line, presumably by the recipient

Chapter VII

13 D U Stiùbhart: <u>The Life and Legacy of Alexander Carmichael</u> p.178

14 It is not easy to determine whether Harvie-Brown accepted Carmichael's views on Gray, but, in accordance with the latter, he did note (Harvie-Brown & Buckley 1888 p.ix) that 'Mr Gray's personal experience of the Outer Hebrides was confined to two or three short visits made in his business capacity as bank inspector, and a fortnight's detention in North Uist'

15 A rather cryptic note, apparently written by Harvie-Brown, is added to this letter: 'I don't know where A.C. has extracted [the] enclosed from [the?] MS. This work is likely to make one use irreverent & irrelevant language'

16 As with some other letters, lines have been drawn through the text, on the first, third and second last pages of this letter

17 Harvie-Brown & Buckley (1888 pp.170-171) remarked only on the slowworm: 'Not rare in some localities, but local in its distribution.' They also noted that 'The Frog and the Toad are unknown in the O.H., and we have no positive records regarding the Lizards'

18 Harvie-Brown & Buckley (1888 pp.36, 36a-d, 37) began the description of rats, black and brown, with a note on Carmichael's observations: 'Mr. Alexander Carmichael informs us that this species [black rat] still exists in Benbeculay. He says: "I saw them about our house at Creagorry several times, and also at Gramsdail, on the opposite side of Benbeculay. I liked to see these pretty creatures, so glossy and black. I never felt that repugnance to the presence of this native rat that I have always felt to the presence of the brown Hanoverian rat"'

Chapter VIII

Letters from John Finlayson

'I had a gold crest in my hands'

There is much in common between this chapter and Chapter 7. However the writers of the letters transcribed in each, Alexander Carmichael and John Finlayson, differed markedly, although they shared an interest in island birds, both were Gaelic speakers, and both were flattered by the attention given to them by John A Harvie-Brown, to whom they wrote. It is therefore of some interest to contrast and compare them through their letters as correspondents of the mainland naturalist.[1]

John Finlayson is said to have been a native of the West Highland village of Lochcarron, otherwise known as Jeantown. He was, it seems, born in 1830, two years before Alexander Carmichael, and was one of a family which, at least in later days, lived in a small terraced house at the west end of the village. Probably by 1850 the occupants of that house could look across the road to a recently built Free Church. A younger brother, Alexander, born in 1833, is better recorded than John, and his earlier career may serve as a guide to the first stages of the less well-known but similar story of John's association with religion.

According to the account of him published in 1898 Alexander attended a school opened by the Free Church in the later 1840s. Thereafter he went to the Free Church Training College in Edinburgh, and then, not liking the prospect of teaching as an occupation, he moved to the University of Edinburgh, where, having completed his studies, he was in due course licensed by the Free Presbytery of Edinburgh. Almost immediately, however,

Chapter VIII

Alexander Finlayson (centre) doctor at Munlochy, Black Isle

he discovered that 'by nature, taste, and social instincts he was unfitted for the work of the ministry', and so determined 'to devote himself to the study of medicine'. Here any parallel religious steps shared by the brothers came to an end, for Alexander took up the medical life and settled eventually at Munlochy on the margin of the Black Isle where by 1898 he had lived and practised for twenty years. In the absence here of a photograph of his elder brother one showing Dr Alexander and two companions is included.[2]

Thus the first stage of John's life matched that of Alexander quite closely, but it happened that little or nothing did after that. With the influence of the 'Disruption' around them, an early enthusiasm for Free Church affairs (quite natural given the disposition of their parents), a Free Church school at hand and a Free Church building erected close by, all this meant that their youthful years until about 1850 had much in common. But then their ways parted. The influence of the Free Church launched John, when a young man of 26, out to the remotest Hebrides, in order to establish a school on Berneray, Mingulay's neighbour to the south. On the voyage through remote and difficult tidal seas John, and whatever fellow crew members were with him, were overtaken by bad weather on their way to that island, and the boat conveying them there had to take shelter in the lee of Mingulay. As a curious and interested visitor John took the opportunity of going ashore. In consequence of meeting the population, entirely Catholic, he was encouraged to set up the intended school there instead of Berneray. Perhaps out of a missionary impulse as well as by the people's strong persuasion, he was to spend much of his remaining life as teacher in Mingulay. In the circumstances he probably maintained an inward attachment to the Free Church doctrine, but at the same time he seems to have enjoyed an often appreciated place among the Catholic islanders.

Chapter VIII

Head and other stations, and I with Bass Rock, Ailsa Craig, Hoy Head, and the Blk [Black] Craig of Stromness, and Handa we had no hesitation in considering it, the most thickly populated of any we had ever beheld. From a gap a few yards further to the northward, we admired the wild grandeur of the rock scenery, excelling in this respect also, – but enough in its praise here. I feel sure it only requires to be better known, to be more fully appreciated, and it certainly should rank first in Scotland [*scarcely*] both as regards its scenery and its population by sea birds. On the summit of the Stack was a fair sprinkling of G. B Backd. Gulls, and a small Colony of Herring gulls also occupied part of the slope facing the Atlantic. The Bridled Guillemot seemed to be in equal proportions as observed at Barra Head. Ravens nestled in the cliffs, and an immense bird flew almost into our faces as it suddenly topped the edge of cliff near which we were sitting. A Peregrine was observed pretty far out at sea flying in a southerly direction and making for the cliffs toward the south end of the island.

'The cragsman brought up about 150 Guillemots and 50 Razorbills eggs from which we chose about 50 of the best. A few of these were really handsome specimens. The Cliffs around on this island do not seem to be as a rule thickly populated with sea fowl but by far the larger seem to have crowded to the ledges of the stack and its immediate vicinity. A bridled bird was brought up.

'We now retraced our steps to the bay where we landed and soon after again set sail for Castle Bay.'[3]

❖

It was no doubt as a result of personal contacts at this time that John Finlayson acquired an interest in the natural environment surrounding him on land and at sea, but it seems, from the absence of any trace of correspondence between Finlayson and Harvie-Brown for over a decade thereafter, that there may have been no further communication between them until the mid 1880s. Their first letters to each other were apparently those of 1887, when Harvie-Brown was busy collecting material for his projected book, <u>A Vertebrate Fauna of the Outer Hebrides</u>.[4]

A new school was established by the Barra School Board and opened, with John Finlayson as teacher, in 1875. It was from this building that Finlayson wrote to Harvie-Brown on 22 March 1887 and again in April of the same year:

<u>22<u>nd</u> March /887</u> *Minglay pub School, Barra, by Oban*
J.A.H Brown Esq.

Dear Sir,
I, at once on opening your kind letter recalled your visit to this Island in /70 and how I had tethered a man down the rock to procure for you a few Specimens of the Guillemots eggs.
  You would likely have heard then itself, that the Lighthouse boatman, who landed you on and off this Island the same day and also ferried you on to <u>Uist</u>, has been drowned the same evening on his return to <u>Barra</u>. He foolishly took the west side and came into contact with sunken rock. It is a man from this Island that was with him. They all perished as well as the dwarf that was with them. Your wish to send you a "list or lists of fish brought into Barra" I do not well comprehend, unless it means a list of fishes brought into Barra for purposes of propagation, and if it means that I really do believe that none were ever introduced

Chapter VIII

for that purpose. I consider there are fewer species of fish found in the waters of the west side of Scotland than in those of the east side. <u>For instance Sprat is never fished for on the west coast, especially on N. west.</u>[5]

   <u>*Wishing you every success*</u> *in your labours and that the yacht will afford you opportunities of enjoying more and more learned curiosities in the Hebrides.*
Your obedient Servant
John Finlayson

And then:

<u>*9th April /887*</u> *Minglay pub School, Barra, Oban*
J.A.H.Brown Esq.

Sir,

I was not a little annoyed by the fact that though having read your kind letter over & over several times, I never noticed the writing on page 4 of it, till two days after I returned you an answer, your having signed your name in the middle of <u>page</u> *3 led me to suppose there was no writing on the back. You wish me to send you notes on the birds of Minglay.*

   I confine myself to the four following species

Guillemots	=	*Langidh*	*in gaelic*
Razorbill	=	*Dubhianach*	= *blackbird*
Puffin	=	*Peta ruadh*	= *red pet, Local*
Kittiwake	=	*Seigir*	

These birds arrive on the Barra coast early in Spring and occasionally visit the rock, making a short stay on it each time till they permanently settle on it about the middle of May when the laying commences. The rock is then taken possession of by two birds for each egg, only that the husband is of necessity absent while procuring food for the wife and the little fellow when it breaks the shell. On special days, perhaps states of the weather, the number of birds in the rocks are more than trebled by the visitation of millions of fellows who act no part in the responsibilities of either father or mother. Of this addition to the inhabitants of the rock the Razarbills predominate.

The guillemots are the first to appear and that in February. The Guillemots sit on the egg quite closely packed and squeezed tight. They lay on large shelves. In a good number of cases, they lay on slopy shelves. It seems from this that the bird is never destined to stir off the egg, for as soon as it does so, the eggs invariably roll over and perish. The male attends to the wants of the female. It is on that account, lean and light, while the other is sottish and fat to an extreme. It is a very silly bird. It often allows itself to be caught by the hand, but that only at the time the young one is nearly being hatched. It and Razarbill are so blinded by attachment to their young during the week before and the week after the little one is hatched that they allow themselves to be captured in hundreds. The way of catching them is by a lasso of horsehair stuck to the top of fishing rods. The Guillemots can carry only one fish at a time with the tail sticking out. The Razarbill and puffin carry as many as 12 or more small herrings every trip. All of them lay several times again when the egg is lost. I have seen the same shelf robbed of its eggs three times. The time allowed between each lifting would be 15 or 16 days. Razarbills hatch quite isolated, they are too vicious to suffer contact with a neighbour. Puffins burrow, never

Chapter VIII

hatch exposed. They are the last to get their young ripe for emigration. Their young ones are fully as big as their mothers before they leave. Guillemots and Razarbills young ones are about the size of the blackbird when they leave. The Puffin cleans out his nest before leaving and can never be captured by the lasso. The Kittiwake begins early in summer to build a nest of mud and weeds. It builds it in ugly slopy places so that heavy rains sometimes do carry away their nests and all. The loss of their first nest compels them to be the last to leave with the young. The time required for hatching is about 4 weeks. The birds leave as soon as ever the young ones [flap?] off the rock. Every single bird invariably sticks to the very spot of rock every year. The Guillemots and Razarbills cannot rise on the wing if they happen to fall on the ground and lose sight of the sea. In foggy weather I have often seen them, in crossing above the Island, found in the hill. They could never rise, only flap and paddle. The people here kill their birds with a heavy pole. They sit on the verge of the rock and the birds come hovering above and within blow distance. No blow on the body can disable the bird. The least knock or blow on the head or neck finishes it, but no blow, however hard, can kill it outright. It is apparently dead when it falls down, but if the neck is not broken, the bird will soon recover. I have seen me give them sore beaks and they would at once make for the water as a cure seemingly. The moment the little ones open their eyes on the world they are as sensible of danger as a man of 60. They invariably keep off the danger side of the rock. Petrel's nests used of old to be found in the rents of peat banks, but none now.

[Yours truly?]
John Finlayson

Please excuse my hurried imperfect notes.

Note at head of second side: *Guillemots and Razarbills all leave Minglay by the 1ˢᵗ August, leaving a majority of the puffins behind and all the kittiwakes. Every bird leaves as soon as ready, that is, as soon as the young one jumps down.*[6]

❖

Harvie-Brown's decision to compose a book on the natural history of the Outer Hebrides largely derived from his adventures in the islands which he generally reached by means of his first yacht, called the *Shiantelle*, built at Fraserburgh in 1887 and given a name seeming to reflect the pleasure of his recent visits to the Shiant Islands in 1879 and 1887. It happened therefore that his first journey to the 'Shiants' was not made in this yacht but in a small boat hired from Tarbert only as far as Scalpay, and then by 'the Fishery yacht *Vigilant*, which looks after the fisheries of the Long Island'. When he went back there in 1887, as he did also to Berneray and Mingulay and to many other islands, he was accompanied as usual on his Hebridean expeditions by the geologist, Professor Forster Heddle of St. Andrews, and by W Norrie, photographer, of Fraserburgh.

Finlayson met Harvie-Brown, and probably his companions, on each of the landings in Mingulay, in 1870, 1871 and 1887. They were duly impressed by each other. Harvie-Brown wrote of their meeting in 1887 as follows:'We spent a happy and enjoyable day in Mingulay, in company with our friend Mr Finlayson, to whose good companionship and genial conversation we owe a good deal of the information gleaned otherwise than by eye.' First-hand knowledge of seabird life on an island also pleased Harvie-Brown, as it did in the case of the kittiwake:

'Speaking of this species, Mr. J. Finlayson, schoolmaster at Mingulay (whose knowledge of the native bird-life is accurate, and is the result of continued residence amongst their haunts), says: "The Kittiwake begins early in summer to build a nest of mud and weeds. It builds it in ugly sloping places, so that heavy rains sometimes carry away the nests. The loss of their nests, I believe, compels them often to be the last of the rock-birds to leave with their young. The time required for hatching is about four weeks. They leave as soon as ever the young ones fly off the rocks. Every bird returns to the exactly same spot of the cliff every year, and this remark applies also to the other species of rock-birds.'"

As his second letter (9th April) shows, Finlayson responded to postal requests from Harvie-Brown for information on wild life, especially birds. These requests were sent to a wide variety of long-term and occasional residents in the Outer Hebrides such as lighthouse keepers and sporting enthusiasts on seasonal visits, and this was a practice of value to other volumes in the 'Fauna' series, which in due course covered most parts of Scotland. Unfortunately none of Harvie-Brown's letters to Finlayson seem to be available and therefore their content can at present only be imagined from what is known to have been their purpose and from what Finlayson said in his probably more friendly replies.

19th aug 1887 Minglay School (by Oban)
J. A. H Brown Esq.

My Dear Sir

I take it for granted you are ere now making gradual but sure progress in the direction of Winter Quarters. I understand you made no stay at Barra after leaving us, for none of the people of this Island saw the yacht lying at Castlebay.

 I have the greatest pleasure of stating that on the 8th or 9th of this month <u>Keith Johnston</u> sent me per parcel post, two valuable volumes of a <u>botanical</u> <u>atlas</u> and another one on British birds. What a heart's Content in them! I take it to be that his issue to me of such fine books, is the result of <u>one</u> or <u>two</u> suggestions by your noble self, while on this Island the other day, you said you would favour me by the issue of such books. A real favour it is and one for which I can never pay you or find anything like words adequate to express my gratitude and indebtedness.

 The books are perfect ornaments, side by side with a great store of Science.

 I am sure you will be sorry to have to part with your kind friend Prof. Heddle. What amiable gentleness about that Gentleman. My best respects to him.

With kindest regards to you
Your humble servant
John Finlayson

❖

Chapter VIII

the end of Aug. I believe they migrate south with their young as soon as they are strong enough. The pipits, starlings and wrens are then our only permanent denizens.

Some of the Wheatears staid this year till near the end of October. About the end of Sept. a colony of Linnets reported themselves. They are here yet, perhaps they will not go farther south. Will see about that. Early in Winter arrived the song thrush, not in large flocks though. Large flocks of Larks arrived at the same time and after a few days stay, left us, perhaps, for the South. We have a few Common Buntings just now. I believe that they and the Larks that came on us in Winter are none of those that left here in Aug with their young. They must be northerners on their way south.

A few Blackbirds arrived. I saw a female one on the 13th. The yellow hammers have not, but they will before winter is over. The Bernicle geese came long since. I asked one of the neighbours could he tell me what big birds were there on the hills. He said that they used to call them "Danish Thrushes", which I believe is quite applicable. These are the Fieldfares and they seldom come here, except when the weather goes to nonsense in their own country.

We seek the signs of the times that, a seat in the Cabinet is not one of blessed ease or Security. Gladstone wants to die in harness and a battle. The weather we have since Nov came in might be called grass growing weather.

Hoping and wishing you will have every success,
your humble Servant
John Finlayson

J.A.H.Brown Esq
Larbert

Finlayson's next letter to Harvie-Brown was rather unusual. It followed his previous one probably early in November 1887 after what he felt was a distinctly greater gap of time than had been the customary interval during the year of their meeting. Moreover, it was only roughly dated. A speculative '1888 ?' was pencilled in much later on under this 'date', below the address at the top right corner of the opening page, and this, being so imprecise, leaves it open as to where the letter should be placed in the sequence of correspondence. Nevertheless the assumption that it was written somewhere in 1888 seems justified on the basis of such internal evidence as the reference to 'the publication of your work' which could only imply the 'Fauna of the Outer Hebrides' volume. Even this, in its context, was not precise enough as it does not necessarily indicate that the book had been already published, an event which occurred late in the autumn of 1888. Other remarks from Finlayson in his reply suggest that this letter was written in the early spring: he refers to 'The winter just past' and its placid quality; and his concluding hope that 'you and your's are all well' indicates that Harvie-Brown was at that time, so far as he knew, in good health, whereas in his letter of 19 March 1888 he expressed concern at the news from Harvie-Brown that the next trip aboard 'the Shiantele' might be hindered by possible development of asthma.[7]

Chapter VIII

Minglay School Barra, Oban

[1888 ? pencilled in]
J.A.H.B.Esq.

Dear Mr Brown

The fact that I have not written you for a long time back, needs not be taken as meaning that I have forgotten you; far from it. I shall never be guilty to that effect. I sincerely trust, then, that you are now fully as full of hope and life as you were when we had the great pleasure of last meeting, you ashore on this <u>Patmos</u>. The Inverness paper, in announcing the publication of your work, mutilated your name, that is, instead of Mr Harvie Brown, it had for the author Mr <u>Harvey Burns</u>, of course the surname Burns does not sound so pleasant to me nor strike the same chord. I have seen the names of your friends, celebrities, Messrs Jolly and Carmichael, among those on the plat-form of a petty land-league meeting the other day in Glasgow. Some of the crofters are rascals inasmuch as they take advantage of the present agitation in order to non-payment. But the day of account is nearing, and some of them really deserve it. This is my experience. In addition to what I have already said about birds, I have very little to state. I met one Jack-daw on the top of the schoolhouse in January. This is the first one I have seen here or anywhere. I never saw one of them at Lochcarron, though plenty rooks are there. I came across one fieldfare in February. This poor one must have been left behind when the others took their flight. This was too bad of them, to have thus dealt so cruelly. I never witnessed so many <u>thrushes</u> on the

Cliffs of Lianamull, Mingulay

Chapter VIII

I never saw them mixing. It appears from this, that the two classes of hares lived in distinct and separate ranges. The white hare, as you know, is not so longlegged. If there are white hares in Lochcarron, I cannot tell.[9] The only land animal in Barra is the otter, of which there are many. As long as the otter can get any of the salmon species, or an eel or rock fish, it never meddles with any other kind. It knows very well the fish in which fat and substance combine. Is it a fact, that the otter closes its eyes while eating? I heard it from men who witnessed the operation. There are no serpents or lizards whatever in the Long Island, unless in Lewis. Many attempts have been made in Barra to grow wood but no growth. Fifty percent of the plants die and those which remain make no apparent progress.

[Of two pages separated from their appropriate location, it is possible that one may be placed here, to continue and conclude this letter.[10] It therefore follows:]

This is the 27th. I was hoping that my letter would get away yesterday, but a snow storm having broken out, interfered. We generally have more snow here in Spring than in winter. Spring is invariably colder than winter. We never heard how you liked your trip to St Kilda or was a trick played on the minister like that by an Inverness photographer who took his negative while the minister was absorbed scanning a monkey let loose among the people. He never consented to have his likeness photographed. This is March the [18th ?] My letter cannot get off Today as the storm is so persistent. The last season was a failure in the <u>mushroom</u> harvest. Perhaps you know that very wet weather is not in their favour. Unless an over saturated soil caused their failure, I don't know what else, June and August were so wet. As a curative for minor disorders of the stomach, mushrooms are a panacea. I found them so. They were so scarce last season that I have had not one meal complete at a time.

The Bernicle geese pass the nights on Lianamull and Arnamull. They feed through the day over the Island. The next day after you left this Island for St Kilda the parent ravens had an onslaught on their children. I think the squabble continues some days. I don't know how long. The result is, that the young ones must yield and leave, and live outside their parents jurisdiction. Such parental treatment!

Boat going [this evening the 19th ?]

Yours Sincerely
John Finlayson

[Note at head of first page] I almost forgot to thank you for the Xm card representing the wistful watchful angler. It came in due time. We have summer sunshine and calms. I cannot say when a boat leaves.

[Presumably written before the page covering the spring snow storm.]

The work of preparing his Outer Hebrides Fauna for publication must have been the main concern for Harvie-Brown in the summer of 1888 when he was on the first or second expedition to the Outer Hebrides, and apparently to St Kilda, in his new yacht *Shiantelle*. But in June of that very year his mother, Elizabeth Spottiswoode, died quite suddenly. Since she was the last of the

Chapter VIII

seven generations of that surname to own the ancient Stirlingshire estate of Dunipace, near Larbert, where she and her only son lived, the event was not only a personal loss but also raised the issue of inheritance. Finlayson was away on the mainland in the early autumn, and happened to pass Dunipace with the intention of calling in, but did not have the nerve to do so. As a consequence he did not respond to what he later declared was very sad news until the beginning of October, and his letter began a new phase in his correspondence with Harvie-Brown:

4th October /88 Minglay-school, Barra, Oban
J.A.H. Brown Esq.

Very dear Mr Brown

I beg to state that I felt very deeply with you in your hour of sore trial and bereavement.
  It is a great mystery to me – I hope you will clear it away – whether or not the people at home knew where to find you at the time your dear mother was struck down. You might be on the high seas at the time. I was so sorry that your tour was so unexpectedly cut short and that by such sad news from home. Did you arrive before dear mother departed this life? Believe me, I was sore and sorry for you when I noticed the death of mother in the obituary. You then needed the consolations of the Gospel of <u>Christ</u>. I have some delicacy in telling you that I was in Glasgow about the end of September. It was my hobby since you left here that I should spend a few days at Dunipace. I was looking on it as an honour that I got an opportunity of doing so. I find that I cannot master a shyness which is natural to me and which is really my

besetting Sin; perhaps your being in trouble kept me back partly. I was very sick in passing your place without seeing you. I want the right cheek and manliness which I greatly deplore. I just look upon my journey to Glasgow as a <u>blank</u> because I did not visit you, Sir.

I wanted the courage but not the <u>will</u>. It may be my last chance on this <u>stage</u>. I was at Larbert going North at 10 o'clock on Tuesday 25th. It is a great pity that through backwardness I could not have enjoyed a blessing which I so much desiderated. I sincerely hope you will excuse me for this backwardness of mine.

Mrs Knight the benefactress of this Island is very sorry for your loss. She also lost her husband last summer.[11]

This Lady is very <u>sanguine</u> about the photographs you have taken in <u>Minglay</u>. I suggested to her that there was a chance of her getting them from you – that you promised me some of them. I dare say your trial and bereavement for a time kept back their execution. We would greatly appreciate some of them if possible

Dear Mrs Knight is keen for them.

How did you come on with the priest of St. Kilda? I was so sorry that your merriment was so short lived.

I trust you are now getting over the blow that, may be, shortened your tour. Please tell me how you passed through your affliction? It is all a mystery to me, how you got on. I hope I shall soon hear an explanation. I saw a Mr Murray here with a <u>yacht</u>. He had his wife and two daughters with him. His wife would be a lady.

and degenerated. I was a tyro in the business. The directions given were rather ambiguous. A short time in a light press I could not understand. I pressed them for 24 hours and then removed them to another paper Quire where I kept them pressed for ever by something like 2 lbs weight. There are five umbels – two kinds of hemlock. The subordinate one grows on the walls of the houses. Its leaf is like the carrot's. The root is poisonous. We have the wild carrot and yarrow or milfoil. The fifth umbel is a tall slender stalk which children are fond of chewing when it is young and tender. Its gaelic name is <u>iuran</u>. I wish I knew the names of all the specimens. It is a valuable store for the Botanist. It is only in a few instances that I dried two of the same species.[13]

Please write me when you get them and tell me every thing about your health. I am more composed about you now than I was last year, when you kept such silence. I have just begun looking over the Register of Marriages in the <u>Scotsman</u>, in hopes of having the very great pleasure of seeing your honoured name mentioned, signifying that you were led to the <u>altar</u>.

May God bless and guide you.
I am, Dear Sir, your faithful and Humble Servant
John Finlayson

Changeable weather kept our letter back from the 7th till this day the 10th. I am going to Castlebay Today. This letter and parcel (flower) will be leaving Barra on the 11th – you should get them on Saturday 12th

Yours very Sincerely
John Finlayson

At some point between early October 1889 and the beginning of the following March Finlayson took on different work at Rodel in Harris, partly as manager and care of the water bird flocks in the winter sporting season, and chiefly to serve the gentlemen guests who came for the shooting. Since this was his twelfth or thirteenth year of such employment, his interest in birds and other wild life had become well known to local people. On this occasion two men visiting the shore nearby brought him a type of bird unknown to them for identification. Within a week or so the bird, a bittern, along with an example of some pressed flowers, arrived by post at Harvie-Brown's door, where both received a better welcome than Finlayson had feared. The bittern was almost certainly added to the collection at Dunipace.

<u>3rd March /90</u> *Rodel, South Harris*
J.A. Harvie Brown Esq.

Sir

I Send you a bittern that was got on the Shore here by two men it was that weak that it let them catch it and it being a Strange bird to them they brought it me to See if I Knew what Kind of bird it was.

You will See Some barley and meal in the bill they were trying to feed it. I have been twelve years in Harris and never Saw a bittern or heard of one being Seen or got and never saw or heard of one being seen or got in any part of Scotland where I have been. Please let me Know if they have been got so far north as this – frequent the Sea Shore.

Chapter VIII

I thought they were always an Inland bird if you have no wish to keep the bird please Send it to Mr Sword curator of the Smith Institute Stirling

I am yours Very Truly
John Finlayson

<u>12th March 1890</u> Rodel, Isle of Harris
J.A. Harvie Brown Esq.

Sir

You are quite welcome to the Bittern. I am Very pleased to hear that you would like to keep the Bird.

I only mentioned to give the bird to Mr Sword if you did not want it yourself. I did not write to Mr Sword about it.

I am Very Sorry to Say that the water fowl are getting Very Scarce. The rarest of the ducks and geese have wandered away and died . The agents of the estate takes no Intrest in them and Lord Dunmore is abroad. They Stopped feeding them all last Shooting Season as they would not pay any person to look after them and I was constantly employed with the Shooting tenant So when he left I began feeding again and there is a few of them gathered back again but I found a great many of them dead about the bogs and I am afraid them that went out to the Sound has little Chance to come back Mostly every crofter has a gun now. There is hardly a boat goes to sea now without one or two guns abord. We had two gentlemen here all last winter and we were often in the Sound of Harris after geese and wildfowl and they were very difficult to get at owing to so much Shooting. The geese wont let a boat near an Island. The only way we could [get] at them was taking the mast down. We have got a Very good Shooting tenant, a Colonel Percy. he has had it this last two Seasons and he has taken a four years lease of the place.

I am Sorry to hear of Rab Finlaysons death I never heard of it before

I am
Yours Very Truly
John Finlayson

<u>12th [March?] 1890</u> Minglay School, Barra, Oban
J.A.H. Brown Esq.

My Dear Mr Brown,

Basing my claim of right to the privilege of writing you, upon the fact that you always invited me to do so whenever I liked, I write you this time after a very long silence, made doubly longer by a keen longing on my part to hear what you are doing and how you are, I hope the flowers proved a <u>success</u> in having a name symbolic of each. Mr Somerville kindly sent me his pamphlets on the <u>flora</u> of Barra and S. <u>uist</u>. His analysis is far too <u>Synthetic</u> and enshrouded in a dark cloud, seen through only by the out and out professionals. It is just too scientific and meant only for the <u>great</u> <u>minority</u>. Such Heathenish words composed of Greek and Latin as he uses of course there is no want of Glary about it.

   I have seen two new birds this year that I never noticed before. On 3rd and 4th March, the half dozen birds I observed on the top of the hill could be none other than the mountain

Chapter VIII

<u>9th March 1892</u> [Part?] letter, listing Mingulay placenames and with notes on birds.

Place names in Minglay as given to it by some primitive people. I begin at N.E. point and take them sun-wise, one by one round the coast till I reach a little beyond your own Island Lianamul

9th March 1892

1	Soalum	An Island. We do not know the meaning of the word
2	Sunada	A rock
3	Carastain	A rock from which we fish with a rod
4	Meinish	A point
5	Glamarigu	Name of a gully where we fish
6	Gista	a fishing rock
7	Hisgir	An Island at low water
8	Thiarigu	Name of a gully
9	Gunarsaidh	Name of a narrow gulley
10	Horaid [Haraid?]	a rock close to above
11	Suidhlish	a little bay where you landed
12	Hilibrig	a shelf for fishing from
13	Bilibibish	a rock for fishing
14	Annir	a landing place
15	Eari	a point
16	Tremisgu	a gulley
17	Seigu	is a fishing place or rock

18	Ogran	a rock where we fish or sit with rod
19	Sgibasdal	a landing place
20	Hesigu	a gulley
21	Gierum	an Island. There are two of them
22	Luthairc [Luthaire?]	a big stack resting on a pedestal in the sea
23	Ginish	a point
24	Rubanish	a point
25	Catarsaidh	a perpendicular rock
26	Hoaspa	an inclined rock
27	Dorlin	An isthmus, fortified by masonry, telling of days of violence
28	Gonamul	two big stacks joined to main Island by trap rock necks
29	Arnamul	an Island
30	Sunigir	a grassy plot at top of a rock
31	Bla lin	The grassy run at base of Aonig
32	Aonig	the high cliff
33	Lianamul	an Island
34	Gursaidh	a high rock opposite Lianamul
35	Ciasigu	name of rock; you notice the termination *gu* in many words – perhaps it should be *ga* like Hecla. The people here sound Hecla as Heclu – a is a scandinavian termination
36	Hona	a rocky point
37	Analep	a rock face

Chapter VIII

one. The general colour is black and pure white. It is black above and when flying it shews colours exactly nearly like that of the oystercatchers. I call it when on the wing nothing else than a miniature oystercatcher. I had it in the latter part of winter feeding in the mud on the verge of the rock. There is more mud at the landing place here than is in the whole Island and that explains its visits to this particular spot. It allows me to go within a stone throw. I do not remember any thing particular about it except the black and white colours. I am not sure whether there was any thing peculiar about its breast. I think there was. I'll look better again. What bird is it? Is it the Knot? or the sanderling or the <u>phalarope</u>? It flies fast and over the sea when disturbed. The grey one does not do that. It flies above the rock. This black and white bird left me early in spring. I saw the grey one yesterday. If you understand what birds these are, please, inform me

Yours faithfully
John Finlayson

<u>17th Oct. 1892</u> *Minglay, Barra, by Oban*
Dear Sir

Apparently you are by this time homed at Headquarters, though, with greater safety you could linger on longer in the course of the Spey than in your former stations.

   I hope you are pleased with the result of your observations there. I have to tell you of many birds that I have seen here since I saw you last. I am sending off your <u>Schedule of observation</u>. *Since May I observed gold finches white throats, chiff chaff redstarts and Black Cap on [5?]th october. It*

allowed me to get as near it as almost to handle it. I thought at first it was a disabled bird but no! It was very agile in catching insects. I was pleased to meet it. The fishermen at Barrahead were one day chasing a non-descript sea duck. It was the upright tail feather that attracted their attention. This would be non other than the long tailed duck of the pole. We are getting very rough weather here in Sept.
The potatoe crop is a failure this year on this Island and so was the mushroom product. I said last year that the kind of weather which was favourable to the production in profusion of mushrooms was also favourable to the potatoe well being. I took three years to prove this. The potatoe and the mushroom <u>fungi</u> must then bear the one upon the other.

   The cold over saturation of June would probably have something to do with the killing of the mushroom seed. I only met with three or four good ones. The herring fishery in Barra last season was a complete blank, more so than ever. This will no doubt lead to the entire abandonment of the Barra station. The curers have been ruined some of them paying out above a £1000 in bounties alone. The crofters of this Island have been severely punished by the land Commissioners for their stiffneckedness in not having paid a penny of rent in the last <u>decade</u>. The assessors found a good large grazing Island with a large stock on it. The reduction of rent was only 10% and they made them pay £198 of arrears. The average reduction in the rent of the other parts of the west Highlands and isles will be about 35%. In Barra it was 37½ of a percentage. Purple sandpipers are citizens of this Island till about the end of March. These have not come here yet. Turnstones came in August. I saw a chaffinch this morning.

   I have been at Oban during the week ended 24th June. I saw the Shiantelle at anchor in the bay. I understood she was out for hire for earning her daily bread.

no exit but the door. I would then if I could, in order to have a sense of security, have an exit or port in the back wall of my bedroom leading to a fire escape fixture. Other people have such additions to their buildings.

The people of this Island are again hopelessly in arrears. The few who used to pay regularly don't pay now, because they find that those others who dont pay are not punished or evicted. Want of discipline is a great fault in this instance.

J.F.

Finlayson's next letter, two years later in the summer of 1899, was substantially his usual record of non-resident incidental birds calling in at Mingulay, some familiar, others unrecognised. There were also notes of his beloved mushrooms, some general island news, and comment on the state of the island flowers that now claimed a good deal of his attention. Perhaps of the most interest to the present account is his reference to a visit the previous year by a 'Miss Freer from London', who was without doubt Miss Ada Goodrich Freer, author and member of the Society for Psychical Research. A small group of Society members visited Mingulay in August 1898 as part of an investigation into Highlands and islands second sight. They attended Mass in the unfinished chapel on the island, along with what Miss Freer described as 'Almost every adult' in Mingulay 'except a retired Presbyterian schoolmaster', certainly John Finlayson. Miss Freer had more to say on him:

'The schoolmaster interested us greatly. He was a scholarly man from the mainland, and could speak English. He came to the island somewhere about 1860, and the story is told that on his arrival the children crowded round to see the school they were going to have! I believe he has never been away; he married a woman of the island, and after teaching for, I think, over thirty years, was pensioned, and now is "passing rich" on half the income of the village preacher. His little croft supplies him with food and clothing; his house is well-furnished with blankets, his fire with peats; and his one luxury is tea – which he imports – of the very best. He has books, and is quite an accomplished botanist, having observed and classified the flora of the island without knowing the names of a dozen flowers.'

She added that 'We had the privilege of being of some use in naming his collection'; and then turned to a collection, not of flowers but of traditional tales, with which, according to his letters, Finlayson had little or nothing to do.

<u>24th August 1899</u> *Minglay, Barra, Oban*
J A H-Brown Esq.

Dear Sir

Most glad was I on receipt of your unexpected letter and that you are still engaged in your favourite pursuit. I wonder how you feel on the destruction of your collection. Such a stern disappointment indeed. I wonder would a person studying supernatural as distinct from natural theology be disappointed to such an extent. It is nothing but the old story repeated, for me to mention here the birds of passage which visit us year by year on their way from high to low latitudes and vice versa and of which I began to take notes after the first <u>trip</u> of the Shiantele to this Island. I may however give their names here again. They are fieldfares siskins snow-buntings redwings redstarts goldfinches greenfinches blackcaps stonechats chaffinches purple Sandpipers and turnstones. In severe

Chapter VIII

weather the sandpipers come up among the houses pecking at something in streams. They are not shy. Sandpipers and turnstones make a long stay on our coast. We have woodcocks and snipes all winter. But outside the above species I have now two <u>cases</u> to relate which may surprise you. It is this. I was on 19th April /97 sitting in the Kitchen, when I heard a slight fluttering on the top of the stair and looking up I saw what I took for a huge butterfly. The girl went after it and caught it in the bedroom. She took it down in her hand. I looked at it. It at once suggested a humming bird so diminutive was it. It was just the veritable <u>gold crest</u>. Such a small being. I could hardly handle it. What moved it to come in to house? Dr McRury told me that soon after, Mcgillivray shot one at Eoligary. The other case is that of a Dipper which came across me in winter. It stayed here a week, never moving any distance from the stream where it found its food. When I disturbed it and made it fly it made no angles with the water way but fly in a line with it. This one at least has not fed on salmon ova during its stay here. What took it here, for the river courses of the Highlands are its home.

The mushrooms are very intermittent in their genesis. I saw none or very few last year. One would suppose that this last summer would have a good yield in August. It is yesterday that I met with a few thick mellow ones. I find they are better before they fully develop. The crows or starlings spoil many of them. They turn them over and put their beaks through them. I don't think the starling is strong enough for the job. Could you devise for me any means of destroying crows which commit <u>havoc</u> among our hens in the hill. They take out all the eggs. No one can get at them with a gun. We have tropical heat in August. We lost all our Cabbage here this year. The stem and roots are attacked with white sluggish small worm. It might be finger and toe. I never before heard of cabbage being attacked.

The Barra herring fishing after many years of failure has this last summer proved a great success. A few curers I believe have been ruined by the high price at which they bought, as high as £2.15 per cran. The west side of Barra is not teeming with gannet anything like what it was in former years when the atlantic was full of herring. This season the young puffins were in such a lean condition as to be unfit for the Kitchen.

I remember one year when all the birds were not eatable. There was no more juice in them than in a piece of straw, even the dogs would not eat or touch them. This should be owing to the scarcity of spawn in fishing grounds. I have seen as many as six trawlers at work here in the bay. They worked for months and Caught every flounder. It is not worth their while to come again in a hurry. It is said that they have not met with such place for flounder in Scotland. The parish Council of Barra dismissed Dr McRury. It is a pity the power the law put into the hands of benighted Crofters. There is a big church built here worth £600. The money has been given by one of the merchants (Glancy) who died last year. If I had been the priest I would try to get a lease of the people as well as of the church for the reason that Lady Cathcart cannot help evicting the people of this Island some day or another for their non-payment of rents. I may state that I am now master of one hundred flowering plants. Last year I had the assistance of Miss Freer from London. It is a pleasure to be able to address any flowers I meet in two names. The book I have on plants is by the author of British birds.[16]

Chapter VIII

The best condition of the mushroom is a short time it spreads. It is then that I find it thick and sweet.

With best wishes
yours Sincerely
John Finlayson

<u>over</u>

What other bird we have here each winter. It has all the habits and movements of a wren, popping in and out between stones but much larger and dingier. The ravens are still here and their annual fight with their grown-up young.

JF

Excuse all defects. I know there are a few in the Composition. I have nothing now to do but to play and admire nature
[At head of letter]: <u>File</u> <u>O.H.</u>   Annals Oct.99

Having presumably spent another winter season at Rodel, though not certainly with any sporting tenants in residence, Finlayson, still there, wrote of Harvie-Brown's forthcoming 'new Volume', which could have been that published in 1904 – <u>A Fauna of the North-West Highlands & Skye</u>, but given Finlayson's erratic dating it might have been another even earlier than the composition of his letter of 1901. Equally uncertain must be the 'book' that 'had such a fine sale', which might have been any of those in the period from 1888 until 1899

15th April 1901 Rodel, Obbe, South Harris, N. B. [Printed address, along with separate heading: 'Telegraph Office: Obbe']

J.A. Harvie Brown Esq.

Sir

Your letter to hand a few days ago. I am Very happy to hear from you. I cannot express to you how Sorry I was to read in the newspapers of the loss of your fine collection of birds by fire a few years ago. I wish you every Success in your new Volume and I am glad to hear that your book had Such a fine Sale. I have referred Several gentlemen to it to our winter Shooting tenants. We had it let the last three winters before this. I am Sorry to Say that Colonel Percy did not manage to get it let this winter. I Cannot Say that I have Seen any new birds in my district Since I was Corresponding with you before and I have had every opportunity as the last three winters we was every other day on the Sound after wild fowl. I am Sorry to Say that wild fowl are Scarcer than they used to be and Very difficult to get at owing to the Crofters and Cottars having So many guns now there is hardly a boat goes to Sea without a gun or two in it so the wild fowl are learning to take very good Care of them-Selfs. <u>Please dont make this Public</u> as it might be against the letting of the winter Shooting.

All the water fowl are away from rodel Loch. Most of the foregin [foreign?] duck died and the others made there way to Sea. We have Some of the geese till a few years ago but the Farmer was Complaining about them and Lord Dunmore requested the Factor to take what was left of them up to Luskintyre. The Crofter[s] has about killed all the half tame

Chapter VIII

Lord Cottenham had the winter Shooting of 1899 – and 1900 they were Shooting hinds December and Januray and did not go after woodcock and Snipe till Feb and only for the house there bag for the winter 35 hinds, 38 woodcock and 98 Snipe with a few various.

The best man for you in North Uist is Mr Andrew McElfrish Lochmaddy he is a Stirling man served his time in Mr Campbells the Fiscals in Stirling – he is Sheriffs clerk in Lochmaddy has been about 15 years there he is a Very Keen Sportsman and used to get a great deal of wildfowl Shooting and takes a great Intrest in your work – the gamekeeprs name is Donald Coul Sponish Lochmaddy. Mr McElfrish is your best man.

Begging to be excused for overlooking your letter I beg to Remain

Sir
Your obedt. Servant
John Finlayson

J.A. Harvie Brown Esq.

[At head of letter: OH. S. Harris]

Finlayson's letters in 1901, mainly from Rodel, kept up his regular accounts of birds shot, others incidentally noticed, and those occasionally added to 'Lord Dunmores wild Fowl'. His mention of never keeping 'any list of Vermin Killed' sounds like a response to Harvie-Brown's record of a 'List of Vermin Killed' which he had received from Mrs Platt at 'Eishken'. References to 'Vermin' raise questions of what creatures counted, in late Victorian times, as 'vermin' at all. Those listed by Mrs Platt's head keeper and seven assistants in 1898-1899 are interestingly named, but not all of which would be on such a list today. Would John Finlayson have accepted peregrines, and old and young ravens?

'Cats – 38
Old Crows – 52
Young Crows – 11
Old Hawks – 11
Young Hawks – 16
Old Ravens – 21
Young Ravens – 29
Peregrines – 2
Falcons ? (by J Ross) – 3
Rats – 234

<u>30th November 1901</u> *Rodel, South Harris*
J.A. Harvie Brown Esq.

Sir

Your letter of the 23rd received as regards Pochards breeding in Harris they may have been escapes from Lord Dunmores wild Fowl or they might have been the young of them as the old birds were quite Strong on the wing and all the wild fowl were Pinoned So they could not have been any of the 2 Pair of Pochards that Lord Dunmore Put down and that Season that they bred there were a lot of Pochards on Loch osigarry all winter. I never Saw a Ptarmigan in my district but I heard the watcher in the Forest describe a bird that he saw on Luskintyre he Said it was like a grouse but white and gray I Suppose it would be a Ptarmigan from north harris there were a few there at that time about 90 or 91.

Chapter VIII

They were Common Pintail that were Interduced – I never Kept any list of Vermin Killed I beg to Remain

Your obedient Servant
John Finlayson

<u>26th April 1902</u> Obbe

[?] Harvie Browne

Sir

Your letter received

I have waited on the Dunara as long as I can. We have Lord and Lady Coltenham [Cottenham?] at the Spring Fishing for this Six Weeks They have gone to borve last night, and I expect them back to rodel this evening So I will have to go back to rodel I am Very Sorry that have not had they pleasure of meeting you.
 Dr. Fletcher of Tarbert is the only party I Know of that will be able to help you he is fond of the gun and I hear that he is the Son of a Game Keeper any notes on Vermin of Intrest I will be only to happy to Send them to you
 Hoping you will have a pleasent tour and that it will do you good I beg to Remain

Yours Faithfully
John Finlayson

[Note at head of first page: <u>O H</u> Sea Trout Kelt fishing]

3<u>rd</u> <u>April 1903</u> *Minglay Island Barra by Oban*
J A H Brown Esq

Dear Sir

I herein enclose for your inspection a <u>Rara</u> <u>avis</u> shot on this Island on 2nd April. I am sure that the find will be very interesting to Naturalists, as it must bring a message. It would likely have been driven on to this Island by the alarming storms of the past five months
   My opinion is, that the bird is the Gyr-falcon. It can be none other according to the book's description. When caught the <u>shrill scream</u> was a duplicate of the peregrine's. I am sure, that at one period of your time, you would be glad to get hold of such extraordinary visitor. It is all white below, white and black spots above. The length is that of the male gyrfalcon.
   The man who shot and sends it to you expects some remuneration for his trouble. I write for him because it is for you. Though I address you here, I am not sure whether you are in the flesh – there being such a long time since which I heard anything of you.
   Alarming storms of persistent fury raged here with few intervals of peace since the beginning of winter – the store of disturbance oscillating from S.E. to a point near west. It is at this point that it reached something like a cyclone and threatened to carry everything before it. The Barra ling fishing used to be well on by the middle of March. This year at the end of March it is <u>nil</u>.
   The people of this Island still hold out against rent payments.

Chapter VIII

The thing is, the management is lax and weak, so that the Crofters become spoilt children. Last year they received per post legal citations to appear before the Sheriff. They never answered. This conduct brings the law into disrepute in the eyes of the crofters.

Last season not one mushroom came above board, though the weather seemed favourable. The mellow fungus is very intermittent in its growth. I know 112 flowers here now. It is 75 I sent you first

John Finlayson

[Note at head of letter: O H since Pubn. To Annals   April 1903 fr July 03]

<u>27th *April 1903*</u> Minglay Barra, Oban
To W Ross & O H

J A H Brown Esq.

My dear Mr Brown

I am so very glad having you still in the land of living mortals.
    It was no wonder should you suppose me dead, Knowing, as you ought to, that a half wink from you would receive a prompt response from me. My only chance about you was, that if there was any thing wrong I would have seen it in the papers. For your sake I was in the habit of ransacking all the items in the Scotsman about the County of Stirling. But in vain. Not a word of you in Denny or anywhere.

The coincidence in our mutual anxiety as to the supposed non-existence of either of us in the present life was rather amusing. Ours were dreams that did not come true. As to the badger, the familiarity and acquaintance with it shown by the old people of Lochcarron pointed to its being in evidence there at some time or other, however remote. The people spoke of it as the stinking badger, hibernating with its nose quite close to the <u>anal pouch</u> and living on its own offensive smell. There was not the least doubt of its existence. The wild recesses of the mountains of Applecross and Torridon would be a favourite retreat for it. The proprietors, in the olden times kept a hired man specially for the destruction of noxious <u>vermin</u> and <u>carniva</u>. This man was called the forester, but in gaelic he was called the Brochdair and the badger was called the Brochd. The Brochdair then means the man that was to grapple with the badger or brochd. I dont think they would invent these gaelic terms without reason. If Calum brochdair lived now he would be the best man for you to see. He was the forester there when I would be 12 or 14. He is not alive now then.

The badger may have got extinct like other animal life and indeed except bad climate and weather all living things are on the decrease. Its a mere fraction of bird visitors I observe in the past decade as compared to the number in evidence before then. Where is now the abundance of fish on the coast of this Island when I first came to it. It is it and the sport it afforded that fascinated me, not the people. We are now starving without fish in the past 6 or 7 years. The cod the lythe and the saithe and many others have taken wing. The cod shoal swims shy of Barra in the past 6 years. The same complaint comes from Scandinavia. In my younger years the rivulet at Lochcarron teemed with trout. Not any now. The *introduction of the sheep might cause this. If you ever had seen a badger when stuffed and dressed you might get a clue to its habitat. It might be in the possession of some Highland chief.*

There was a sharp fight here the other day between three ravens. Two against one. This one would be a stranger lately come. He might perhaps be one of last year's brood come to visit the old haunts and here the parent pair got at him. One of the pair left about the middle of the fight and left the husband to deal with the stranger. They were better matched now. The stranger when put into a corner would fight stubbornly on the ground with seeming advantage. If it knew its own superiority in fight the other one would fare badly. But it was too much of a coward. The poor thing alighted within a few feet of me. How it panted. It knew well enough that to settle down on a door step would give it relief from attack. But where has the one of the pair that left gone. Yes, it went to take care of the family in the eyrie. You may be able to recall that I showed you that eyrie

At this point the letter comes to a halt, and if its continuation is on one of the detached sheets it may well have been the following with a pencilled '27 April 1903' at the top right hand corner of a headless letter starting at p.5:

I was one afternoon last year fishing, sitting on the rock by the water side with a high wall of rock behind me, when suddenly there were a swoop and pounce on a kittiwake sitting on the sea a few yards in front of me. This was the peregrines pounce. I was glad it missed its aim. It grazed close on its quarry but failed after all. It would probably have seen my long fishing rod after it passed my line to the front. Coming from the land it would never see me till it passed me to the front. Something would be wrong with it. It could easily have taken up the bird but stopped when it noticed me. Nothing surprised me more than the action of the kittiwake. It got up and soared high and higher till it reached more than the height of Aonig rock. It so acted perhaps fearing a renewal of the attack. But the peregrine left without any more attempt.

It is marvellous how birds big and small got trained such as to know that their only chance of life lies in the power of surmounting the enemy. Often have I seen the pipit rise up trap by trap, bafling its sworn enemy.

Every chance I got of noticing the sparrow hawk giving chase, there was nothing of the climb up in it. It would be a zigzag race, but for this tripping by the small bird, it would be captured at once.

I wonder whether the Minglay eagles died or emigrated. J man told me Today that he saw an eagle take up a lamb. He thinks there were no ravens then. The advent of the raven might cause the disappearance of the eagles. It is the arrival on this Island of the puffin that caused the departure of the birds that were here formerly. The old people told me that these birds were fat and good to eat. These might be the fulmars. They were so good for the table that McNeil the chief had to be supplied with some. When I came here forty years ago, there were two ring plovers nesting on the sand near the village. I am annoyed by the voice of a non-descript bird in the dusky twilight of autumn overhead and on the wing. One or two notes are all that I hear. I listen but there is no more to be heard. It puts me in mind of the Curlew's but sweeter and more sonorous. Somewhat like the note of the ring plover but

Chapter VIII

The natural law by which some British birds leave their breeding stations in winter is absolutely unerring in its aim as to their safety. Why then, are exceptions in the divine law which sends the snipes to this Island to perish through the means intended for their preservation. The thing is, it is rarely that we have a week of continuous frost, so that after all it is not a mistake for the snipes to winter here. I have seen a year in which it was a mistake. The snipes are very scarce here this winter. There are more woodcocks. I mind a year when a number of woodcocks were found floating on the sea between this and Barrahead. They would likely have perished by striking the Lighthouse.

It is only one properly migratory bird I met in October and that was one fieldfare.

I dont call chaffinches or stone chats birds of passage. They come here any time in winter when they are hard pressed at home.

The restless hedge sparrow paid me a visit lately. I dont see it now. I had your purple sandpipers as companions at the sea wash when angling in Nov. I dont see them now. Where have gone the red-starts, siskins snow buntings redwings blackcaps fieldfares that I used to meet with.

I had a gold crest in my hands.

A girl here the other day was scarefied by the appearance of a big grey bird with a cat's eyes and head. I went to see could I get a sight of it but failed. This would be an <u>owl</u>. Its <u>note</u> was a scream. The girl got within a few yards of it. The lass startled. What has become of the birds that passed to the south in Oct. and Nov. Always a fewer number called on their way north than did on the way for the south.

I may state that the herring fishing in the western Lochs of Inverness and Ross is a failure this year. This is certainly owing to the depopulation of the Minch in summer by no less a number of boats than 2000 between Barrahead and the Butt of Lewis. Before the east coast boats began their work about Lewis, there would be plenty herring found in some loch or another but the shoals are now scattered and kept back by an impregnable barrier of net work. We are also so beset with trawlers east and west, that the hook is shelved. Not a day but we have trawlers on our shores. They are doing <u>havoc</u>. I may say that the Barra folk used Dr McAulay meanly. He was dismissed by a plebiscite of savages – So also was Dr McRury. There is a new Dr now. It is those dishonest people who never pay a Dr that are always Keen to dismiss him.

There is a good deal of persecution in the business. The spirit of popery has been from the first intolerant. Their weakness Keeps them down. Papists are far from being loyal to the British succession. When the priest puts on the paraphernalia he is equal in power to the Deity. To deny that would be to deny the efficacy of the power of the priest in the confession.

That crack brained Marquis of Bute thought that by sending part of his heart to Palestine, he was securing for himself everlasting salvation and that other pronounced fanatic, who though born a Duke is not on that account in the least iota less an ass or fool than a street arab, Captaining a gang of gullible cringing mortals on a pilgrimage to <u>Rome</u>. What do you think of the fiscal Boom?

Balfour [and?] Chamberlain are my favourite politicians. Communication on the high seas between ships widely apart by Marconiism beats the record.

I wonder what will be the next explosion (Boom) from <u>latency</u> I was sorry that on the eve of leaving for Ross, you had

Chapter VIII

to answer my letter in order to send money to the crofter for the gyr. If this day were yesterday I would not have written to trouble you

With best wishes
yours,
John Finlayson

The native of Barra is to be an idolater and spiritual slave till the millennium. He must think as others direct him. They were so jubilant here at the sudden collapse of our King as to satisfy themselves as to the certainty of god's cutting him down for the coronation <u>oath</u>. *But thanks to god for the disappointment*

 It is when there are many species in the same genus of plants that the distinction is puzzling

 We have the leaf of wild chamomile and scurvy grass (cochlearia) in a flourishing condition in winter.

 I know 112 flowers on this Island now, one or two which I dont know, I was expecting to send to <u>Trail</u> *for identification, but I never sent. There was a badger captured in Badenoch last summer. There were two distilling plants captured at Loch Torridon side likely at the time you were there. Did you see any thing of it*

J F

A detached sheet of a letter, with a pencilled date – 20 April 1903 – at the top right-hand corner, could well, with its tone and topics, belong to this item and so is given here:

I might state that no papist is loyal to British success or the succession. That brainsick imbecile The Duke of Norfolk heading 19 British s[c?]ottish peers in their unholy pilgrimage to the feet of the pope.

I am satisfied about my flowers. There is some difficulty when there are many species. We have here three geraniums. I know them as a tribe only. There is one with a long beak, others with straight short beaks. It is only two flowers on the Island I cannot identify. I don't know how to get them known.

The boat is leaving. I must close up. Your's still living

John Finlayson

❖

John Finlayson's letter of 26th December 1903 to Harvie-Brown was his last. News of his death was conveyed to his naturalist friend in a letter from Morag Campbell Finlayson, adopted niece of Finlayson and his wife, Jane Campbell. The letters written from Mingulay and Rodel after 1900 told their own story of the retired teacher's final few years when he raced from subject to subject and thereby kept up most sides of his contact with Dunipace. In the concluding two or three lines of that December communication he mentioned his knowledge of more than a hundred island flowers, his intention to ask a botanist, 'Trail', to help in identifying two or three which puzzled him, the capture of a badger in the Badenoch district of Strathspey, and two illicit whisky stills discovered in Torridon – a not unusual 'capture'. Then Morag shyly took up the picture of her deceased 'Uncle':

Chapter VIII

[July/Aug. ?]13th 1904 Minglay Barra by Oban
J. Brown Esqr

Sir

It is very sore with my heart indeed that I have to tell you that my dear Uncle Mr Finlayson died on the 22nd March. I am his adopted girl and for his sake I do write this note but I know right enough it is too much for me to think to write to you Sir. but however I will try in Chance as I like to let you know about our sad news.

I am sure you will be very sorry but great alas to us there is no help for it.

I am staying with my dear aunty Mrs Finlayson she is very old looking as she is awfully bad with rheumatism in her foot she cannot walk a step without a stick. I heard my very dear Uncle many a time speaking about you and specially when your house was burned down he was in an awful [stiad? state?] at that time. I remember quite well that I saw you in our house long time ago now and also on seeing your yacht.

I am thinking it was on sunday you went up to our house. I know quite well about the little hook you have put in my shoulder shawl it was in our house for a long time after. please excuse me for this letter as I know it is very far back for a gentleman, but I hope it will do in the case.

I may say we have a very poor and most lonely house after the my dear and warmest friend ever I met and I do not think to meet the like of him again in this world and I am quite sure of that. I am thinking I shall ever remember on him till the [end] of my life.

But I hope God almighty will pay him for his kindeness to me.

Indeed he was more a father to me than Uncle. I have spent twenty years along with him. I came to his house at two years of age, and so I am very far down and put about after his death. I am aunty and is always hearing from his only brother and we are really very [plesand?]

I hope you will excuse this note as I said too much but I cant never stoping speaking about Mr Finlayson.

My aunty joins me in good wishes to you Sir but I am afraid it is too much for me.

Morag Campbell Finlayson
c/o Mrs Finlayson

<u>24th Aug. 1904</u> Minglay, Barra
J.A H Brown, Esq.
Dunipace
Larbert

Dear Sir,

I received your kind letter four days ago, and the parcel containing Boracic acid, Boracic Lint, and oiled Silk.

Mrs Finlayson and I offer our sincerest thanks for your kindness.

I have acted according to your instructions, last night and applied the wet Lint to Mrs Finlayson's foot, but the pain has been for so long a time in the joints, that some time shall elapse before the removal of the pain can be expected.

Chapter VIII

We have every hope that the Boracic Acid shall relieve the pain.

I will soon write to you again and let you know the result.

I have been looking for Mushrooms for Mrs Finlayson and only got half-a-dozen after a whole day's search. The cows are very fond of them, and leave none. They seem to know what is good for them.

The doctor at Castlebay just now is Dr. Taylor. He is an old man, and is only a year at Castlebay.

Dr MacAulay is in South Uist.

Again thanking you for your kindness.

I remain
Yours truly
Morag Campbell Finlayson

7<u>th</u> April 1905 Minglay Barra
J.A.H.Brown Esq.

Dear Sir

I am most glad to say by now that my Aunty Mrs Finlayson is wonderful better with the good stuff you so kindly sent her long time ago, she is sometimes using it yet , but I am sure she shall never get clear of the pain alltogether as she is too old.
I am thinking that she shall be ever thanking you in her heart day and night, and also a young man a friend to myself he was in a very bad state last month with his two knees and he tried some of it and in two days he was able enough to walk through Minglay. And now Dear sir as we can never pay you, I beg to offer you a thousand thanks. We shall be ever indebted to you

for your kindness as I know no one would do anything like that to us.

Dr. Taylor was not on the Island since he was at Mr Finlayson just a year last fortnight, and that year was a lonely one to us. We spend the winter months lone[l]y and dull but I hope summer shall get us releif as we shall be like prisoners during the bad weather. also I hope to get away from Minglay soon as I cant stay but I am very sorry to say that it is so very unhandy. I am thinking we shall be better in Castlebay

Please excuse me for this note. Trusting this shall find you well and happy.

Yrs sincerely
Morag Campbell Finlayson
Minglay

PS. Mrs Finlayson joins me in thousand good wishes

Thus, with good will and the best of wishes, ends the life and memory of John Finlayson, told by himself, by John A Harvie-Brown, Miss Freer, Morag Campbell Finlayson, and perhaps a few others.

Appendix

In the section on the <u>Common Guillemot</u> in their <u>A Vertebrate Fauna of the Outer Hebrides</u> [pp.160-163] J A Harvie-Brown and T E Buckley included a lengthy passage based on what John Finlayson had sent Harvie-Brown in his letter of 9th April 1887. This passage runs as follows and may be compared with the letter:

'Speaking of this species, along with the Razorbill and Puffin, Mr. John Finlayson, schoolmaster at Mingulay, says: "These birds arrive on our coasts early in spring and occasionally visit the rock, making a short stay upon it each time, till they permanently settle upon it about the middle of May, when laying commences. The rock is now taken possession of by a population of birds representing two birds (male and female) for each single egg. The one bird is of course, and of necessity, absent, providing food for the other, and when the young are hatched out, for them also. On special days – perhaps states of the weather – the numbers of birds "in the rocks" are more than trebled by the visitation of millions of fellows, who act no part in the responsibilities of either father or mother. Of these additions to the inhabitants of the rocks the Razorbills predominate. The Guillemots are the first to appear, and they come in February. The Guillemots sit on their eggs quite closely packed one against another, and choosing the broadest shelves. In some instances," continues Mr. Finlayson, "they lay on sloping shelves, and in such cases it seems that the birds are destined never to stir off the eggs, for as soon as they do so the eggs invariably roll over the edge and perish.

The male attends to the wants of the female, and in consequence is lean and light, while the latter is sottish and fat to an extreme. The female often allows itself to be caught by the hand, but that only at the time when the young one is nearly being hatched. The Guillemots and also the Razorbills are so blinded by their affection for their young that, during the week before and the week after the little ones are hatched, they allow themselves to be captured in hundreds. The way of capturing them practised in Mingulay and Barray is by a lasso of horsehair stuck to the top of fishing-rods. The Guillemot can carry only one fish at a time with the tail projecting, but the Razorbill and Puffin carry as many as twelve or more small herrings every trip. All the species lay several times again if their eggs are lost. I have seen the same shelf robbed three times of its eggs. The times allowed between each lifting may be fifteen or sixteen days.

"Razorbills hatch more isolated from one another. They are too vicious to suffer contact with a neighbour. Puffins burrow; never hatch in exposed situations. They are the last to have their young ripe for migration. Guillemots' and Razorbills' young are about the size of blackbirds when they leave. The Puffin clears out his nesting hole before leaving. He can scarcely ever be captured by the lasso.

"Another method followed at Mingulay," continues Mr. Finlayson, of capturing the birds, is also "by means of a heavy pole. The natives sit on the verge of the cliff, and the birds come hovering above and within blow-distance. No blow on the body appears to disable the birds, but the least knock or blow on the heads or necks finishes them, though no blow, however hard, kills them outright. They are apparently dead when they fall down, but if the necks be not broken they will soon recover. The moment the little ones open their eyes on the world around them, they are as sensible of danger as a man of sixty. They invariably keep away from the danger side of the rock." Finally, Mr. J Finlayson tells us: "Guillemots and Razorbills all leave Mingulay by the 15th of August, leaving a majority of the Puffins behind, and all the Kittiwakes."

References and Notes

(Endnotes)

1 This account of the background to John Finlayson's letters to Harvie-Brown relies to a large extent on probably the only two recent published works devoted to Mingulay: <u>Mingulay – An Island and Its People</u> by Ben Buxton Edinburgh 1995; <u>A Window into Life on Mingulay; Extracts from the School Log Book 1875-1910 – Contributions by Ben Buxton and David Powell</u> Edited by Bob and Shirley Chambers. Kershader, , Isle of Lewis 2012

2 <u>The Celtic Monthly – A Magazine for Highlanders</u> Vol.6 pp.225 and illustration opposite 1898. Dr Alexander Finlayson is the central figure.

3 Harvie-Brown: <u>Journal 1870 pp. 246-248</u> The Journals are part of the Harvie-Brown collection in the library of the National Museum of Scotland, Chambers Street, Edinburgh

4 This significant year 1871was also the occasion [September or October] when two men who became known as the most noteworthy of the folklorist collectors in the Hebrides were, like John Finlayson a decade earlier, forced to seek shelter in Mingulay – John F Campbell of Islay and Alexander Carmichael [Alexander Carmichael: <u>Carmina Gadelica – Hymns and Incantations</u> Vol. II p.352 Edinburgh 1928 'In October 1871, the late J. F. Campbell of Islay and the writer were storm-stayed in the precipitous island of Miunghlaidh, Barra. We occupied our time in listening to the folklore of the people by whom we were so kindly treated']

5 The tragic drowning episode described briefly in this letter was also recorded by Harvie-Brown in his journal p.251 – Tuesday 31st May 1870, under a page head title of 'Poor Rory McPhees death'. Rory and possibly 'his man' lived on Mingulay.:
Dunvegan C. [Castle] came in ¼ past 1. p.m. Arrived at North Bay. There I met Mr. Maclennan manager for Barra. He gave me the most distressing news, viz that Poor Rory, his man & boy, were all lost during their return voyage from Pollochawe [Pollachar]. The pieces of the boat were found on Sunday but no trace discovered of the bodies. Rory leaves

Ireland – Dingle Peninsular, Blasket Islands	1963	
Taransay	1964	
St Kilda	1966	7 May – 27 May (with school party)
Rona	1966	28 July – 19 August
Taransay	1967	12 August – 17 August
Harris	1967	17 August – 28 August
Gàisgeir	1967	31 August
Haskeir	1967	1 September
Soay, St Kilda	1967	1 September – 3 September
Mingulay	1967	4 September
St Kilda	1968	4 May – 17 May (with school party)
Sulaisgeir	1969	29 July
Skye	1970	25 March – 29 March
Lewis	1970	9 May – 22 May
Boreray	1970	23 July – 31 July
Raasay	1972	5 May – 10 May
Skye	1973	7 April – 13 April
St Kilda	1973	5 May – 21 May (with school party)
Lewis	1973	9 July – 1 August
Lewis	1974	27 April – 10 May (with school party)
Harris	1974	28 June – 5 July

Pabbay	1974	
Lewis	1974	6 July – 19 July
Fladda Chuain	1975	
Harris	1975	3 May – 11 May (with school party)
Harris	1975	4 August – 9 August
Lewis	1975	10 August – 14 August
Sulaisgeir	1975	15 August – 16 August
Lewis	1975	17 August – 20 August
Lewis	1976	5 July – 18 July
Harris	1977	14 May – 17 May
Lewis	1978	14 September – 24 September
Colonsay	1981	
Harris and Lewis	1987	24 June – 1 July
Harris	1988	10 June – 13 June
The Shiants	1988	13 June – 18 June
Harris	1988	19 June – 23 June
Harris	1989	17 April – 24 April
Harris and Taransay	1989	27 June – 10 July
Harris	1989	6 October – 12 October
Lewis	1990	5 January – 11 January
Lewis	1990	11 April – 19 April
Harris, Taransay, Killegray	1990	12 June – 21 June
Lewis , Harris, Uist, Eriskay	1992	10 June – 16 June

Publications

Books and Booklets

The Ballads of Liddesdale, Newcastleton 1986, 40pp

(With A.O. Mackie) *The Parish of Linton*, Hawick ND., 16pp

Tibbie Shiel, Newcastleton 1986, 16pp

Ride With The Moonlight. The Mosstroopers of the Border, Newcastleton 1987, 53pp

Sheep of the Borders, Newcastleton 1988, 31pp

An Ingenious Mechanic of Scotland. James Small (c.1740-1793) of Berwickshire and Midlothian, Newcastleton 1989, 22pp

Editor, *No Road This Way After Dark. George Harkness's Reminiscences of Liddesdale*, Newcastleton 1989, 107pp

A Break With The Past. Changed Days on Two Border Sheep Farms (Langburnshiels and Riccarton), Newcastleton 1991, 118pp

Rona. The Distant Island, Stornoway: Acair 1991, 179pp

A Desert Place in the Sea. The Early Churches of Northern Lewis, Habost: Comunn Eachdraidh Nis 1997, 95pp

Surnames and Clansmen. Border family History in Earlier Days, Port of Ness 1998, 200pp

Cornelius Con. An Irish priest in the Hebrides, Port of Ness 2002, 24pp

Editor, *Curiosities of Art and Nature. The new annotated and illustrated edition of Martin Martin's classic A Description of the Western Islands of Scotland*, Port of Ness: The Islands Book Trust 2003, 318pp

Compiler, *The Angus Macleod Archive. An Introduction to the Collection*, Port of Ness: The Islands Book Trust 2004, 56pp

Dykes, Ditches and Disputes. A History of Boundary and Field Enclosures in the Borders, Port of Ness 2004, 100pp

Forts and Fallen Walls. The duns of northern Lewis, Port of Ness 2004, 62pp

St Kilda. Church, Visitors and "Natives", Port of Ness: The Islands Book Trust 2005, 755pp

A Sad Tale of the Sea. The story of Malcolm MacDonald and Murdo MacKay on the island of Rona, Port of Ness 2006, 50pp

Editor, *People of Ness. Some earlier records: Galson to Eoropie*, Port of Ness 2008, 45pp

The Great Forest of Lewis, Port of Ness 2011, 127pp

Articles

The Breeding Birds of North Rona, in *Scottish Birds. The Journal of the Scottish Ornithologists Club* Vol. 5 No.3. Autumn 1968, 126-155

Feus at Teviothead in 1844, in *Hawick Archaeological Society Transactions* 1969, 41-44

An Episode in the History of the Borders. Accusations Against Robert Scott of Harwood in 1663, in *Hawick Archaeological Society Transactions* 1970, 38-53

Notes on the Historical Background and Sources of "Jock O' The Side", in *Hawick Archaeological Society Transactions* 1971, 11-16

Henry Scott Riddell and the Parish of Teviothead, in *Hawick Archaeological Society Transactions* 1971, 22-40

The Story of Gilpin Horner, in *Hawick Archaeological Society Transactions* 1973, 12-19

Sir Walter Scott's Collecting of Ballads in the Borders, in *Hawick Archaeological Society Transactions* 1974, 3-33

The Allanmouth Tower and the Scotts of Allanhaugh, in *Hawick Archaeological Society Transactions* 1977, 12-22

The Letting of the Common Haugh of Hawick 1814-1835, in *Hawick Archaeological Society Transactions* 1978, 3-10

The Saughtree Crosses in Hawick Museum, *in Hawick Archaeological Society Transactions* 1978, 34-39

Early Days of the Society, in *Hawick Archaeological Society Transactions* 1979, 11-18

The Living Voice, in *Togail Tir Marking Time. The Map of the Western Isles* edited by Finlay Macleod, Stornoway: Acair 1989, 97-104

The Chisholms: Highland Names in the Borders, *in Borders Family History Magazine* Issue 28, June 1995

Who was Little Arthur Foster ?/ Elliots at Court 1675-1682, in *Borders Family History Magazine* Issue 29, October 1995 and Issue 30, February 1996

The Parish of Langlands, in *Borders Family History Magazine* Issue 34, June 1997

Update on "Surnames and Clansmen", in *Borders Family History Magazine* Issue 43, June 2000

Why not to live in St Kilda, in *Island Notes* No.1, The Islands Book Trust August 2002

The Name "*Callicvol*", in *Fios* No.112 30 August 2002

Mysterious and Forgotten Placenames, in *Fios* No.113 13 September 2002

Beanntan na Mor-thir, in *Fios* No.114 27 September 2002

The Sea and the Sand. The History of Port of Ness Harbour, in *Fios* No.115 11October 2002

A Brief History of Cuidhsiadar, in *Fios* No.116 25 October 2002

History of Port of Ness Harbour, *Island Notes* No.3, The Islands Book Trust October 2002

The Ancient Boundaries of Ness, in *Fios* No.117 8 November 2002

Land Boundary Markers – a problem in featureless moorland, in *Fios* No.118 22 November 2002

Exploring Placenames in South-east Lewis, in *Island Notes* No.2, The Islands Book Trust November 2002

The Bogs of Lewis, in *Fios* No.119 6 December 2002

The Wild Moorland, in *Fios* No.120 20 December 2002

The Flannan Isles, *Island Notes* No.7, The Islands Book Trust January 2003

"This Wild and Beautiful Wilderness". A 1930's Tolsta to Ness Walk, in *Fios* No.121 17 January 2003

"Lewis places of interest are Callernish, Carloway, the Butt and Gress". Exploring an 1882 visitor guide, in *Fios* No.122 31 January 2003

An Inspector Calls. The Reminiscences of a 19th Century Schools Inspector. In *Fios* No.123 14 February 2003

An Early Education. How the First Schools Came into Being, in *Fios* No.124 28 February 2003

The First Schools. An Enthusiasm for Education in Ness, in *Fios* No.125 14 March 2003

Local Schools in the 19th Century. The Development of Ness Education, in *Fios* No.126 28 March 2003

A Background to Shielings, *Island Notes* No. 4, The Islands Book Trust April 2003

Ladies Schools in the 19th Century. The Continuing Development of Ness Education, in *Fios* No.127 11 April 2003

A New Schoolhouse for Ness. The Continuing Development of Ness Education, in *Fios* No.128 25 April 2003

Leabhar na Feinne. The Work of Malcolm Macphail, in *Fios* No. 129 9 May 2003

Exploring the Antiquities. The Work of Malcolm Macphail and F W L Thomas, in *Fios No*.130 23 May 2003

The Duns of Ness. The Work of Malcolm Macphail and Captain Thomas, in *Fios* No.131 6 June 2003

"Tighean Iair". The Work of Malcolm Macphail, in *Fios* No.132
20 June 2003

Pennylands. The Work of Malcolm Macphail, in *Fios* No.133 4 July 2003

From Craggans to Creels. The Long History of Local Crafts, in *Fios* No.134 18 July 2003

The Antiquarian Attractions of Ness, in *Fios* No.136 15 August 2003

The Secret Stills of Ness, in *Fios* No.137 29 August 2003

Martin Martin, in *Fios* No.138 12 September 2003

The Importance of Our History, in *Fios* No.139 26 September 2003

The Bigger Picture, in *Fios* No.140 10 October 2003

The Colour of Grizzly Bears, in *Fios* No.141 24 October 2003

Island Memories from the 1930s, in *Fios* No.142 7 November 2003

Troubles Over Rona, *Island Notes* No.10, The Islands Book Trust November 2003

St Kilda and the "Outside World", *Island Notes* No.13, The Islands Book Trust August 2004

J A Harvie-Brown in the Outer Hebrides, *Island Notes* No.14, The Islands Book Trust November 2004

Lewis Heritage at Risk ?, in *Eilean an Fhraoich*, Winter 2004

Martin Martin on Uist, *Island Notes* No.17, The Islands Book Trust April 2005

The Great Forest on the other side of Loch Shell, *Island Notes* No.19, The Islands Book Trust July 2005

Bibliography

Barrowman, C; McHardy, I; & Macleod, M: <u>Severe Terrain Archaeological Campaign (STAC) Rope Access and Topographical Survey</u> – Unpublished interim report 2004

Bruford, A J & Macdonald, D A (edits.): <u>Scottish Traditional Tales</u> Edinburgh 1994

Buxton, B: <u>Mingulay – An Island and Its People</u> Edinburgh 1995

Buxton, B: <u>The Vatersay Raiders</u> Edinburgh 2008

Campbell, J F: <u>Leabhar na Feinne – Vol.I heroic Gaelic Ballads</u> London 1872

Campbell, J G: <u>Superstitions of the Highlands & Islands of Scotland</u> Glasgow 1900

Campbell, John L & Hall, Trevor H: <u>Strange Things</u> London 1968

Carmichael, Alexander: <u>Carmina Gadelica – Hymns and Incantations</u> Vol.II Edinburgh 1928

<u>Census Return 1851</u>

Chambers, Bob & Shirley (edits.): <u>A Window into Life on Mingulay: Extracts from the School Log Book 1875-1910 – Contributions By Ben Buxton and David Powell</u> Kershader, South Lochs, Isle of Lewis 2012

Cox, R A V: <u>The Gaelic Place-Names of Carloway, Isle of Lewis</u> Dublin 2002

Daniell, W: <u>A Voyage round the north and north-west Coast of Scotland and the Adjacent Islands</u> London n.d.

Dwelly, E: <u>The Illustrated Gaelic-English Dictionary</u> Fifth Edition Glasgow 1949

Fergusson, Charles: Papers in two parts on 'The Gaelic Names of Birds' in <u>TGSI</u> Vols XI and XII

Gibson, John C: <u>Lands and Lairds of Larbert and Dunipace Parishes</u> Glasgow 1908

Goodrich-Freer, A: <u>Outer Isles</u> London (Westminster) 1902

Gray, R: <u>The Birds of the West of Scotland including The Outer Hebrides</u> Glasgow 1871

Harvie-Brown, J A: 'Further Notes on North Rona, being an Appendix to Mr John Swinburn's Paper on that Island in the "Proceedings" of this Society, 1883-84' in <u>Proceedings of the Royal Physical Society of Edinburgh</u> 1885-88

Harvie-Brown, J A: <u>Travels of a Naturalist in Northern Europe</u> 2 Vols. London 1895

Harvie-Brown, J A: <u>Collection of correspondence, journals, 'commonplace Book' etc.</u> in Library of the National Museums of Scotland, Chambers Street, Edinburgh

Harvie-Brown, J A & Buckley, T E: <u>A Vertebrate Fauna of the Outer Hebrides</u> Edinburgh 1888

Harvie-Brown, J A & Macpherson, Rev. H A: <u>A Fauna of the North-West Highlands & Skye</u> Edinburgh 1904

Henshall, A S: <u>The Chambered Tombs of Scotland</u> 2 Vols Edinburgh 1972

Macaulay, D: 'Studying the place names of Bernera' in <u>TGSI</u> XLVII (1971-72)

Macdonald, D (coll.): <u>Tales and Traditions of the Lews</u> Stornoway 1967

Macdonald, D: <u>Lewis – A History of the Island</u> Edinburgh 1978

Macdonald, D: The Tolsta Townships Tolsta 1984

Macdonald, N (edit.): The Morrison Manuscript – Traditions of the Western Isles by Donald Morrison, Cooper, Stornoway Stornoway 1975

Mackay, C J: Place-Names of Scarp – John Maclennan Stornoway 2001

Mackenzie, C: 'An Account of some Remains of Antiquity in the Island of Lewis, one of the Hebrides' in Archaeologia Scotica Vol.I

Mackenzie, John Munro: Diary 1851 Stornoway 1994

Mackenzie, W C: History of the Outer Hebrides Paisley 1903

Mackenzie, W C: The Book of the Lews Paisley 1919

Macleod: The Angus Macleod Collection Kershader, South Lochs, Isle of Lewis

McCulloch, J H: Sheep Dogs and their Masters Dumfries 1940

Martin, M: A Description of the Western Islands of Scotland London 1703

Matheson, W: 'History of the Macaulays' in SG 1956-57 [Annotated copies in NLS]

Mitchell, A: The Past in the Present: What is Civilisation? Edinburgh 1880

Morrison, M: Fear Siubhal nan Gleann – Orain agus Dain Glasgow (1923 ?)

Morrison, N: Hebridean Lore and Romance Inverness 1936

Rheinalt, Tristan Ap: A Thankless Task? Alexander Carmichael as a collector of Gaelic bird names Kershader, South Lochs, Isle of Lewis 2010

Robson, M: Rona – the Distant Island Stornoway 1991

Robson, M: <u>Forts and Fallen Walls – the duns of northern Lewis</u> Port of Ness 2004

Robson, M: <u>St Kilda – Church, Visitors and 'Natives'</u> Port of Ness 2005

Robson, M: <u>A Sad Tale of the Sea – The story of Malcolm MacDonald and Murdo MacKay on the Island of Rona</u> Port of Ness 2006

Sayce, R U: 'Popular Enclosures and the One-Night House' in <u>Montgomeryshire Collections</u> Vol.47 1942

Sayce, R U: 'The One-Night House, and its Distribution' in <u>Folk-Lore</u> Vol. 53 1942

Seaton, A V (edit.): <u>Journal of an Expedition to the Feroe and Westman Islands and Iceland 1835 by George Clayton Atkinson</u> Newcastle upon Tyne 1989

Smith, W Anderson: <u>Lewsiana</u> London 1875

Stahl, A-B: 'On the Verge of Loss – Leser-Known Place-names of Barra and Vatersay' in A Kruse (edit.): <u>Barra and Skye – Two Hebridean Perspectives</u> Scottish Society for Northern Studies Edinburgh 2006

Stewart, W G: <u>The Popular Superstitions and Festive Amusements of the Highlanders of Scotland</u> Edinburgh 1823

Stiubhart, D U: <u>The Life and Legacy of Alexander Carmichael</u> South Lochs, Isle of Lewis 2008

<u>The Celtic Monthly – A Magazine for Highlanders</u>

<u>The New Statistical Account of Scotland</u> Edinburgh & London 1845

<u>The Royal Commission on Ancient and Historical Monuments and Constructions of Scotland – Ninth Report with Inventory of Monuments and Constructions on the Outer Hebrides, Skye and the Small Isles</u> Edinburgh 1928

<u>The Statistical Account of Scotland</u> Reprint Wakefield Vol.XX 1983

Thomas, F W L: 'Notice of beehive houses in Harris and Lewis; with traditions of the "each uisge," or water-horse, connected therewith' in PSAS Vol.III pp.127-134

Thomas, F W L: 'Description of beehive houses in Uig, Lewis, and of a Pict's house and cromlech, etc., Harris' in PSAS Vol.III pp.134-144

Thomas, F W L: 'On the primitive dwellings and hypogea of the Outer Hebrides' in PSAS Vol.VII (1870) March 1867 pp.161-162

Thomas, F W L: 'Traditions of the Macaulays of Lewis' in PSAS Vol.14 June 1880

Thomas, F W L: 'On the Duns of the Outer Hebrides' in Archaeologia Scotica Vol.V 1890

Thomas, F W L Collection: Orkney Archives Kirkwall

Thomas, F W L: Papers in Library of the National Museums of Scotland, Chambers Street, Edinburgh.

Thomson, J: Map entitled Middle Part of Western Isles Edinburgh 1822

Tocher no.57 Edinburgh 2003

Zickermann, K: 'Scottish Merchant Families in the Early Modern Period' in Northern Studies Vol.45 Edinburgh 2014

Index

A

612 County of Aberdeen Squadron 151
Abhuinn (Amhuinn) Dhubh 95, 97
Adabroc 99
'Admiral Benbow' inn 164
Airidh a' Bhealaich 97
Airidh Dhòmhnuill Chaim 107-111
Airidh Iain Mhic Ailein 92
Airidh na h-Aon Oidhche
 (shieling of one night) 7, 10, 164, 170, 179, 185, 187-191, 194-196
Airidh nan Gearraidhean 98
Airidhean nan Grùigean 98
Alasdair na Sàile Bige 127, 145
Allt a Mhaide 99
Allt an t-Sulaire 93, 95
Allt Chaluim Chille 69, 74, 76
Allt Chasgro 97, 98
Allt Loch Airidh na h-Aon Oidhche 191
Allt na Cloich 82
Allt na Muilne 74, 75, 82, 84
Allt Sheilastotair 99, 100
Am Breabadair Ruadh 136
Amhuinn Chaithaseadair 98, 99
Amhuinn Gheireadha (Garry River) 76, 82, 85, 86
Amhuinn Lidhe 76
Amhuinn Sgiogarstaigh 100

An Gobha Bàn, parish blacksmith (the big blacksmith) 120, 122, 133
An Sgoilear Bàn 117
Anti Surface Vessel (ASV) 151
'antiquarian predilections' 26
Applecross 128, 319, 323
Archer, George (Sergeant) 153
Atkinson, Robert 16, 159, 161, 163

B

Back 69, 73
Baile an Truiseil 43
Bailevanaich, Balivanich etc. 167, 168, 173, 179, 180
'Balgloum' 132
barnacle geese 200
barp 186
Barra 27, 139, 141, 170, 188, 189, 194, 196, 198-202, 222, 223, 238, 250-252, 258-263, 267, 268, 272, 275-278, 280-283, 285, 286, 289, 290, 296-298, 300-304, 307, 309, 317-319, 322, 325, 326, 328-330, 333, 335, 336, 351
Barron, Mr
 (Editor of Inverness Courier) 214
Barvas 14, 17, 20, 25, 35, 43, 45-49, 61, 64, 65, 78, 80, 82, 100, 103, 109, 116, 117, 120, 126
battle of Machair-House at Reef 135

Bayhead, North Uist 189
'beehive' houses 19, 21, 25, 41, 352
Beinn Bhràgair 190
Beinn Gheireadha 82, 84
Beinn Mheadhanach 76
Beinn nan Caorach 76, 79
Beinn Rathacleit 190
Beirigh Bheag 112
Beirigh Mòr 112
Benbecula 9, 10, 26, 28, 41, 150, 165, 167, 169, 171, 173, 175, 179, 182, 183, 186-189, 194, 202, 234, 239, 244, 245, 247, 249, 338
Berisay 140
Bernera, Great Bernera 39, 62, 131, 140, 148, 338, 349
Bhata Guaille 99, 100
Bilascleitir ('Fieliskletter') 93
Black Dog 9, 154, 164, 166-169, 171-173, 176, 177, 179-181, 183, 188, 190, 193-195
Black Gate of Bailevanaich 180
black rat 10, 245-249, 254, 282, 283, 338
Bones, Billy (Captain) 164
books 16, 116, 196, 209, 219, 221, 239, 267, 280, 299, 307, 342
boundaries 73, 75, 345
Borve 68, 80, 82, 316
Bragar 10, 98, 130, 145
Brenish 138, 144
Broad Bay 67
broch at Bragar 79, 130
broch at Carloway 79, 133
Bruinigil 108, 109

Buckley, T E 10, 197, 218, 252-254, 332, 336, 349
'Bushy Lake' 22
Butt of Lewis 65, 79, 150, 164, 325

C

Caisteal a' Mhorair 9, 84, 85
Caithaseadair 98, 99
Caithness 151
Calbost 191, 192
Callaige 76, 78
Callanish 44, 46
'Cally, Gatehouse, Kirkcudbright' 212
Cameron, Donald (Ruaig, Tiree) 188
Cameron, Rev. J (Stornoway) 116
Campar Mòr 97-98
Campbell, J F (of Islay) 52, 179, 187, 335
Campbell, John Gregorson 188
Canada 74
Cape Province, South Africa 152
Cape Wrath 153
Carloway district 190, 196, 348
Carmichael, Alexander 9, 13, 14, 25, 32, 171, 173, 255, 335, 336, 338
Carmichael, Alexander 197-254
  Letters to John A Harvie-Brown
Carmichael, Dr 224
Carmina Gadelica 9, 14, 197, 250, 251, 335, 348
Carnan 49, 207
Castlebay 250, 267, 280-283, 286, 330-331
Castletown 152
Ceann na Drochaid 124, 148

Ceapabhal 28, 41
Celtic Societies 29, 212
chain fetter 128
chambered cairn 43, 167
chapels 23, 79, 151, 196
'church of St Aula' 79
churchyard at Baile na Cille 144
Clach an Truiseil 9, 13, 43-65, 109
Clach an Truiseil: conflict near 48
Clach an Truiseil: height 44, 47, 57
Clach Uaine 86
Cladach Chuidhaseadair 95
Cladh Mhìcheil 69
Cleite Beag 76
Cnip (Kneep) 120
Cnoc a' Rainich 85, 86
Cock 71, 123
Colonsay 182, 188, 195, 341
commons, commonties 169
Constable, Mr 239-241, 244
Cornaigmore, Tiree 188
corncrake 206, 242, 253
Cornwall 170
craggan 14, 17, 24, 25, 38, 41, 347
Craig, John Du 139-142, 149
Creag Mhòr 82
Creagan na Mì-chomhairle 132, 136, 148
Creagorry 202, 245-247, 254
Cromore 191, 193
Crowlista 136, 137
Cuidhaseadair 9, 91, 94-97, 99
Cùilatotair 89, 90, 91

D

Dà Loch Fhuaineabhat 76
Dalbeg 146
Dalgleish, Mr 203
Danish pirate at Reef 135, 136, 148
Davis, A C (Pilot Officer) 156-158, 161
Dìbadal 87, 88, 90, 91, 93
Dìbadal Iorach 90, 91
Dìbadal Uarach 90
'Dirishgil' 116
Dixon, Mr (Inveran) 218
Dòmhnull Cam 107-149
Dòmhnull Cam: children 124, 144
Dòmhnull Cam: daughters:
 Ann/Anne, m. Murdo Morison tacksman of Gress; ?, m. Alexander Macleod (Alasdair na Sàile Bige) Dalmore 118, 124, 145
Dòmhnull Cam: death of 144
Dòmhnull Cam: sons:
 Angus tacksman of Brenish, John tacksman of Kneep (Iain Ruadh air a' Chnip), William in Islivig 118, 124, 145
'Donl mac an taillear' 31
Drew (Group Captain) 156
druids 45, 47
Druim Diridean 76
Druim Mioraig 190
Druim nan Cairnan 49
Druim Thallagro 97
Dulochan, at Struan-du-Ruaival 184, 185
Dùn Bhilascleitir ('Dun Villisklet') 93, 106
Dun Carloway: climbing with daggers 134

Dùn Othail 76, 78, 81, 87-89, 106
Dunvegan Castle 115, 129

E
Earrascro 69
Edinburgh Castle 115
Eight Farthings Lands 136
Eilean Glas Cuilatotair 90
Eilghean (nickname) 144
Elwes, Henry J 198
England 164, 170
'Enishgary' 140
Eoligarry 198, 322
Eorodale 99
Eoropie ('Europee'):
   twenty tenants of 72
Eriskay 189, 341
'Errista' 116

F
'Faire na h-Aon Oidhche' 188
Faroe Islands 150
Feadan a' Ghamhna 93, 95
Feadan Dubh 95
Feadan na Maoime 92
Feadan Nighean a' Bhreitheimh 81, 88, 105
Feadan Siorravig 43
Fearchar Dubh 191
Feilden, H W 198, 201, 202
Fergus(s)on, Charles 212-217, 219, 244, 249, 253
Fianuis, Rona 154
Fidigidh 22
Fife Adventurers 125
Finlayson, John (Mingulay) 13, 222,
   Letters to John A Harvie-Brown 255-338
fishing station at Sgiogarstaigh 101
Fivepenny: ten tenants of 72, 97
Flannan Isles 133, 339, 346
Flodda(y), island of 339
Foots, William (Sergeant) 153
Forest of Harris 19, 20
France 170
'Fraoch', poem of 30
Frazer, James
   (bank accountant, Lochmaddy) 206
Frost and Fire 201, 252

G
Gaelic Society of Inverness 11, 211-213, 216-218, 235
Gaick in Badenoch 183
Gàisgeir 18, 39, 340
Gallon Head 142
Gamekeeper 19, 20, 24
Gannet 95, 207, 303, 309
'Garraidh' (a dog) 242, 243
Garry River (Amhuinn Gheireadha) 76
Gayner, Patrick 95, 96
Geàrraidh Bhat a Leòis 89
Geàrraidh Loch Eilleagbhal 89
Geàrraidh na h-Aibhne 190
Geireadha Mhor 86
Geodh' a Ghille 78
Geodh Chaip 29
Geodha Ruadh 109
'George Rona' – deceased person
   found on Rona 158, 160, 162
Gil an Tairbh 81, 90
Gil Bhatisga 93

Gil Dhìbadail 90, 91
Gil Sgibagearraidh 92
Gil Sgiogarstaigh 100
Giordale 69
Glen Rannoch 85
Gormelia (Gormul), daughter of Fearchar Dubh 191, 192
Gramsdail 245, 247, 254
gravel pits 82, 87
graves at Caithaseadair 99
Graviner switch 152
Gravir 191
Gray, Robert 198, 235
Gress 69, 79, 81, 145, 346, 357
Grimersta River 64, 131, 140
Grimsby 166
guillemots 200, 259-265, 302, 303, 332-334
Gunn, Angus 33, 35

H

Hacleit, in Benbecula 167
Harris 9, 18-23, 28, 32, 33, 38, 41, 98, 106, 109, 116, 119, 120, 129, 190, 198, 199, 208, 223, 233, 238, 245, 253, 268, 287, 288, 311-315, 339-341, 352
Harvie-Brown, John A 10, 13, 347, 349
Harvie-Brown, John A
   Letters from Alexander Carmichael 197-254
   Letters from John Finlayson 255-338
Haskeir 250, 340
Hatchwell (Flying Officer) 152, 153
Hatston 152
Henson (Pilot Officer) 153
hill of Tolsta 72

HMS *Mist* 158, 160, 161
HMS *Preston North End*, trawler 156
horse's head 120, 122

I

Iceland 64, 150, 166, 351
Inverness 11, 196, 202, 211-216, 235, 272, 276, 304, 324, 350
Iodhlainn Aonghais Riabhaich 99
Ireland 19, 64, 95, 123, 170, 182, 212, 340
Irish rebellion 123
Islay 198, 222, 224, 233, 236, 252, 335

J

'Jasserie' 170
Johnson, Michael (LAC) 159
Jura, island of 188

K

Kallin, in Grimsay 150
kelp workers 109
Killegray 109, 341
Kilmorack 212
Kindrogan 212
Kirkibost 132, 135-137, 140
Kirkwall 155, 195, 352
Knockard, seven tenants of 72, 73, 99
Knockruagan 50, 64

L

Lady of the Lake 182
Lamont, Donald 238
'Laoidh Chrìosd' ('Hymn of Chrìosd') 31
'Laoidh an Truisealaich' 51-53, 55

Larach Tigh Dhubhastail 24
Lathamor 86
Leub an Darnidar 139
Leaba Phrion[nsa Theàrlaich]
 – 'Prince Charles's Bed' 187
Leigastal 75
letters 13, 197, 203, 208, 209, 213, 216, 232, 235, 241, 250, 254, 255, 261, 266, 268, 285, 298, 307, 314, 327, 335
Lewis, island of 13, 16-18, 20, 21, 23-25, 32, 33, 36-39, 41, 43, 44, 46, 50, 51, 64-67, 69, 70, 78-81, 85, 90, 93, 97, 99, 103, 105-109, 112, 114-119, 124, 125, 127-129, 136, 137, 139-141, 143,147-150, 154, 160, 164, 190, 191, 196, 198, 207, 208, 238, 245, 252, 276, 325, 335, 336, 340-343, 345-352
Leyden, John 188, 193
Lighe nan Leac 78
Lingavat 69
Linshader 50, 64, 131
Lìonal 8, 19, 52, 81, 90, 91, 102, 103
Lismore, island of 25, 225, 233
Loch a Tuath 67
Loch Airidh na h-Aon Oidhche 10, 176, 189-191
Loch an Dùna 130
Loch an Eich Uisge 188, 189
Loch Beag Caitiosbhal 191
Loch beirbh 28
Loch Bharabhat (Barravat) 117, 141, 149
Loch Bhasapol 188
Loch Bhat a Leòis 89
Loch Caol Dùin Othail 76, 88

Loch Claidh 193
Loch Diridean 76
Loch Dubh na h-Airde 109
Loch Eilleagbhal 76
Loch Eynort 189
Loch Langabhat 90, 106
Loch Meabhag 19, 41
'Loch Murnaick' 78
Loch na Craobhaig 22
Loch nan Strùban, North Uist 190
Loch Resort 18, 21, 24, 37, 116
Loch Roag 24, 36, 47, 140
Loch Scarasdail 76
Loch Seaforth 107, 108, 120, 193
Loch Sgeireach 76, 81, 87-89
Loch Sgeireach a' Ghlinn Mhòir 76
Loch Sgeireach na Creige Briste 81, 88, 89
Loch Shell (Sealg) 107, 193, 347
Loch Tamanabhaigh 21
Loch Tana nan Leac 76
Loch Tealasbhaigh 21
Lochlannaich 186
Lochmaddy 25, 190, 197, 198, 200-202, 206, 237, 239, 240, 280, 314
Londonderry 123
Long Island 139, 187, 198, 201, 202, 239, 265, 276
Lorne, Lord 223
Lusbairdean, Lusbardan 182

M

Macaulay, Angus
 (son of Domhnull Cam) 138
Macaulay, Dughall (Dougal) 118, 119, 123

Macaulay, Iain Ruadh 118, 144
Macaulays 33, 49, 50, 64, 115-117, 119, 120, 125, 126, 130, 136, 138-140, 143, 144, 147-149, 350, 352
MacCarmaig, Roderick (crofter Dungaineacha, Benbecula) 183, 185
MacColl, Father Donald 249
MacCormick, Peter (Hacleit, Benbecula) 167, 169, 171, 183
MacDonald, Alexander 30
MacDonald, Donald (Grimsay) 245
MacDonald, Flora 187
MacDonald, John 203, 205
MacDonald, Malcolm 207, 253, 343, 351
MacDonald, Margaret 99
MacGille Eadharain, Fionnlagh 124
MacGillivray, Dr (Barra) 198, 252
MacGillivray, John (son of William) 223
MacGillivray, William 223, 240, 250
Macinnon, James (crofter Bailevanaich) 173
Maciver (McEiver), Roderick (Rory) 70-71
Maciver (McKiver) 69, 70, 71, 75
MacKay, Murdo 207, 253, 343, 351
Mackay, William 213, 215, 217, 218
MacKenzie, John Munro 81, 105
MacKenzie, John Munro: diary of 81, 105
MacKenzie, Mr (Shader) 100, 106
MacKenzie, Rev. 212
MacKenzie, Stewart (Proprietor) 82
Mac(k)innon, Professor 211, 236
Maclean, Angus (Aonghas Mòr Riabhach) 98

Maclennan, John 190, 196, 350
MacLeod, Annie (Stornoway) 170
MacLeod, Murdo (boat-builder and fisherman) 164
MacLeod, Mr Murdo (cooper and ship-owner) 116
Macleod, Neil 126, 127, 129, 140, 141
Macleod, Reverend L. (Church of Scotland, Lewis) 160
MacLeod, Roderick (of Lewis) 125
Macleod, Rory Mòr 115
MacNuaran, Cuoch 135
MacNuaran, Darge 134, 135
MacNuaran, Tid 135
Macphail 148, 188, 194
MacPhail, John Roy 126-128, 130-133, 136, 137
MacPhail, Malcolm 51, 52, 65, 152, 346, 347
MacPhee (shepherd in Balivanich), Macphie 167-169, 187-190, 193, 194
MacPhee: twelve foster brothers of 172
Macphie (of Colonsay) 182, 188
Macrae, Rev. William (Barvas) 48
Macrury, Dr. 234, 249
Maghannan 22
Mangursta 111, 113, 120
Maoim 91-93, 100
Maoldonuich 250
maps 15, 16, 69, 102, 106, 165, 196, 209, 165
Martin, Martin 43, 253, 343, 347
Mas Chaipmheall 29, 41
Mathers, A (Sergeant) 153
Matheson, Sir James (Proprietor of Lewis) 35, 81, 82, 198

Matheson, William 64, 115-119, 122, 123, 125, 126, 143-145, 147-149, 350
McBane 123, 124
McCoul, Mulcallum 115, 119
McCowell, Alister 119
McCowell, Donald 119
McCowell, Donald og 119
McCowell, James moir 119
McCowell, James og 119
McCowell, John og 119
McDonald, Norman 201
McMillan, superintendent foreman of road works 81
McNeil, Donald (tenant in South Tolsta) 70
Merlin engines 156
Mermaid, The – poem by John Leyden 188
Milton 28, 199
Ming(u)lay 10, 222, 257, 258, 261, 262, 265, 267, 268, 272, 273, 275, 278-283, 285, 289, 290-292, 296, 298, 300, 306, 307, 317, 318, 321, 322, 328-336, 338, 340, 348
Mitchell, Arthur 14, 17
Mol Garbh 113
Moll na h-Arde 142
Morrison, Donald (cooper – An Sgoilear Bàn) 35, 49, 64, 115-118, 120, 125, 126, 129, 130, 133, 135, 137, 139, 143, 145, 147, 350
Morrison, Dr Robert 159
Morrison, John (the Brieve) 125
Morrison, Mr 20, 21
Morrison, Peter (crofter and farm constable, Bailevanaich) 179-181

Moss 15, 45, 46, 47, 48, 96, 98, 100, 102, 112, 186
mounds 79, 87, 99, 298
Muir, T S 23, 79-82, 86, 87, 90, 91, 93, 101, 196
Mùirneag 60, 61, 75, 78
Mure, Mr (T S Muir in Leith) 181, 196
Murray, Donald 95, 97
Murray, Kenneth 80
Murray, Norman (Habost, Ness) 51

N

names of birds (Gaelic) 201, 211-213, 216-219, 226, 227, 232, 234, 235, 240
names of fish (Gaelic) 233, 243, 244
National Museum(s) of Scotland (Edinburgh) 8, 42, 253, 349, 352
Ness 13, 16, 33-36, 43, 47, 49-52, 56, 59, 66-82, 86-88, 95-106, 124-126, 133, 137, 138, 164, 195, 207, 208, 253, 342-347, 351
'Nether Lochaber' 212-215
Newton (North Uist) 203, 237, 238, 241-243
Nicolson, Alexander 213
No.63 Maintenance Unit at RAF Carluke, Glasgow 156
Norsemen 49, 68, 96
North Dell 33
North Galson 33, 35, 124
North Rona 9, 13, 16, 49, 80, 89, 150-163, 166, 207-211, 253, 340-344, 347, 349-351
North Tolsta 69-82, 100, 103
North Uist 32, 150, 189, 190, 198, 200, 203, 205, 225, 245, 254, 314

Northton 28
Norway 202, 252
Nunton 28, 41, 237, 239

O

old blind woman 138, 149
'One-night house', ('Ty un nos',
 'Hafod-un-nos', 'Caban-un-nos') 223
Orkney 8, 19, 151
ornithologists 199, 203, 219, 244, 344

P

palmister (fortune teller) 138, 149
Paterson, Mrs (Bearnaray, Harris) 223
Peat 31, 45-47, 57, 75, 81, 89, 96-101,
 169, 186, 264
Pennylands 68, 69, 347
'Pentlands' (i.e. Pentland Firth area)
 152
peregrine falcon 203, 225, 226, 229
Perthshire 212, 214, 217
Picts 186
Pintail duck 199, 203
Pitlochry 212
Poll Thothatom, Rona 156, 157, 161
Port Gheireadha 86
Port of Ness – unfinished harbour 164
post mortem 207
Prìosan Dhòmhnaill Chaim 111

R

Raasay 150, 183, 340
rabbit hunt 125, 126
Raeburn Place, Edinburgh 207, 208
Raigmore 212
'rebellis of the Lewis' 115

Rias 108
Richardson, T M 47
road to Ness 43
Roisinnis 187
Rona, island of 9, 13, 16, 49, 80, 89,
 150-163, 166, 207-211, 253, 340-344,
 347, 349-351
Ross-shire 198
Ruabhal, Ruaival 167, 187
Rudh' Eadar Dha Bheirigh 112
Rudha Fir Uige 108

S

St Kilda 15, 18, 37, 166, 195, 208, 276,
 277, 279, 336, 340, 343-347, 351,
St Michael 68, 69
Scarp 37, 190, 196, 339, 350
Scolpaig 203, 205, 207
Scott, Sir Walter 182, 344
Scottish Privy Council 115
Scrabster 156
Sea eagle 198, 225
seal story 221
Seann Bhaile 69, 70
Seaweed 99, 100
Seilastotair (Heilistotar) 99, 100
Seileir (Cellar Head) 91
Sgealadal 108
Sgeir Dhòmhnaill Chaim 109
Sgiogarstagh 69, 78, 80, 86, 97, 99-101
sgoth (niseach) 73
Shader 44, 45, 48-50, 65, 68, 82, 100,
 106
Sharbau/Sharban/Shaban, Mr 21, 22,
 24
Shetland 151

Shieling 41, 73, 89-93, 97, 99, 107, 108, 111, 167-173, 180, 182, 185, 187, 189-193
Siarem, little isle of 125
Sìthean an Airgid 107
Sìthean a Croer, Rona 154
Skye 33, 38, 105, 115, 128, 129, 150, 187, 196, 213, 221, 237, 280, 310, 337, 339, 340, 349, 351
Slabhcan 39
Slabhucan 39
Slavonian Grebe 200, 203
Slowworm 254
Smeirtam 76
Snaoisval 30
Society of Antiquaries 11, 23-26
Sollas 207
South Beach, Stornoway 141
South Dell 137, 145
South Lochs 10, 117, 191, 196, 252, 348, 350, 351
South Tolsta 70, 71, 74-76
South Uist 13, 27, 30, 181, 189, 200, 238, 249, 330
Sromos 109
Stac Dhòmhnuill Chaim 9, 110-114, 117
Stac na Beirighe 112, 113
Staingeabhal 168
Steall Amhuinn na Cloich 86
Steinacleit 43
Steinnol Beag 191
Stevenson, Robert Louis 164, 194
Stewart, Rev. Alexander 213, 216
Stewart, W Grant 182, 183, 196, 351
Stiarabhal, Stairreval 167, 180, 184

Stone, Arthur (Sergeant) 153
Stonechat(s) *stone-chats* 207, 281, 285, 291, 294, 307, 324
Stornoway 16, 25, 35, 36, 62, 66, 73, 78, 80-82, 96, 103-105, 115, 116, 136, 147, 152, 164, 170, 187, 196, 208, 238, 239, 244, 253, 342, 345, 349
Stornoway, parish of 106
Stornoway Castle 34, 35, 141, 198, 230, 312
Stornoway Gazette 11, 159, 350
Strachan, Rev. J (Barvas) 126
'Strathavon' (Oban) 204
Sulasgeir 80, 151
Sutherland 182, 227, 275
Sutherland, Rev. Mr (Benderloch) 204
Swainbost 49, 103
Sybil, daughter of Fearchar Dubh 191, 192, 193
Sycamore, twigs of 128

T

Taobh Tuath 28
Taransay 18, 38, 39, 339-341
Tarbert 19, 265, 316
Teampull Chanaiseadair 144
Thomas, Frederick W L (Captain, Lieutenant etc.) 17-29, 32, 33, 36, 39, 115, 118, 123-127, 130, 145, 171, 178, 182, 208, 209, 346
Thomas, Frederick W L: notes by 9, 34, 41, 42, 113, 116, 118, 145-149, 195, 346, 352
Thurso 106, 156
Timsgarry 144
Tobar nic Fhearghuis 144

'Tolestaff', 'Tollasta', 'Tolstay' 68, 70, 71
Tolsta Farm 74-81, 87, 88, 103
Tom Fhidagro 95
Torcasaidh 28, 41
Torlum 234
Torquil Dubh 125
Torquil (Torcall) Og
   Torquil (Torcall) Dubh 126
'Torran Mòr' 116
'Tota Gormaig' 80, 101
Totaichean Gheireadha Mhòr 86
Tràigh Gheireadha
   (Tràigh Geiraha) 9, 83, 85
Tràigh Mhòr, Tolsta 76, 105
Treasure Island 164

U

'Uacar', farm in Benbecula 173
Uamha' na Seann Daoine 92
Uig (Lewis) 17, 20, 21, 24, 25, 33, 36, 41, 57, 64, 81, 106-112, 116-120, 123, 125, 126, 129-143, 148, 196, 352
Uist 26, 187, 202, 219, 224, 233, 237, 240, 261, 341, 347
Ullapool 33, 34, 127, 130

V

Valtos 116, 120, 125, 145
Vasey (Lieutenant) 157, 159
Vatersay, Barra 170, 195, 196, 281, 283, 336, 348, 351
Verse 173
Vertebrate Fauna of the Outer Hebrides, A by J A Harvie-Brown and
   T E Buckley 197, 249, 250, 252, 261, 332, 336, 349,

W

Wales 169, 170, 298
Waller, Desmond C F
   (senior N.C.O. (Flight Sergeant) of salvage team) 157, 161, 162
Wallis, John B M
   (Wing Commander, later Air Commodore) 152-162
Watt, Rev. Michael 126
West Loch Tarbert 18, 19
whale 146
Whitley planes 151, 152, 156-161
Wick airfield 151, 152, 155, 156
Wife of Laggan 183
'Winkie' (see Wallis, John B M)
'women with beaks of bone' 180
wooden calendar 210